Instant Wisdom

10 Easy Ways To Get Smart Fast

by
Beth Burgess

First published in the UK in 2018
Published by Eightball Publishing

ISBN 978-0-9573217-3-1

Cover image courtesy of Robert Ellsworth Tyler

Introduction

Do you want to be a smarter, wiser person? Do you want to become an expert at solving tricky problems that used to leave you stuck? Do you want to be able to devise amazingly creative solutions? Do you want to boost your brain's capabilities?

This book will teach you tools, tweaks and techniques that will make you smarter in mere minutes, or even just seconds. They are easy to do, won't cost you any money, and some require no real effort at all!

That may sound incredible, but the strategies I'll teach you are backed by science and include quick and easy methods that geniuses and peak performers use to get amazing results. Whatever your education level or IQ, this book *will* make you smarter.

You will learn:

- Einstein's top tool to be ultra-inventive (you can do this in your sleep)
- The 'Alice in Wonderland' technique that helps you learn anything (it's fast *and* fun)
- A way to boost your creativity that is so simple that kids can do it (it's literally child's play)
- How to fool your brain into being super-focused (an actor used this trick to land millionaire-making roles)
- An ancient technique that will make you much wiser (a famous Greek philosopher's secret weapon)

- How to become cleverer doing things you love (this surprising method leads to happiness *and* success)
- The tactic top athletes use for ultimate performance (but you don't even have to leave your chair for this)
- A delicious way to boost your logic (granny knows this trick, but I bet you don't)
- The 'Smart Stranger' method for achieving instant insight (this is a genius way of solving any problem)
- How to get great minds to improve your intelligence (no reading, money or bribes required)

There is much more than this, but before we dive into it, you may be wondering how I learned these tools. The truth is that I used to be a very unwise person. I wasn't a moron, but I made some dumb decisions that got me into a lot of trouble. I wasn't good at using my intelligence and I came up with some really stupid ways of solving problems.

For example, in my mid-teens, I developed an anxiety disorder. I didn't know what to do about it, so I just avoided situations that made me anxious. Doing that only made the issue worse. So, by my late teens, my disorder was even more serious. I was too scared to even leave my house most of the time.

As things worsened, I became too anxious to seek help, so I smothered my anxiety with alcohol. I never foresaw what a mess my life would become.

By my early 20s, I was a severe alcoholic, practically homeless, and had ruined many of my relationships. My decisions back then got me arrested and chucked into mental hospital and police cells several times. I became so ill that I had to keep quitting my studies and jobs. I lost most of my pancreas due to my drinking and put myself into so many dangerous situations. Goodness knows how I'm still alive.

But after dragging along rock bottom for a very long time, I was finally broken enough to seek help and start my journey to recovery.

As I recovered, I learned how to use my intelligence more effectively – to make good decisions rather than to scam myself out of trouble. I discovered techniques that helped me solve problems properly, rather than just avoiding them.

And the more I knew, the more I wanted to know. So, I set out on a special journey to gain more wisdom and to learn how to use my brain to live a smarter life.

As my life improved, I used the tools to study, to start a business, to create great relationships and to become more productive. And now I want to share what I've learned to help others live smarter lives too.

This book contains tips to give your brain a fast boost when you need it most, methods to make you more capable and creative, and techniques you can use on the spot to gain immediate insight and make wiser choices. You can apply what you learn to all areas of your life. I hope your success and happiness grows as much as mine did – and more.

About the Author

Beth Burgess was a total mess and is now a respected therapist and coach, an avid learner, and a writer.

She is the founder of wiseism.com, a resource to help people use wisdom to improve their lives.

This book is the first in the Wiseism series.

Beth's life missions include helping as many people as possible to achieve a wiser life.

Beth is not a know-it-all, but is keen on researching, reading and experimenting.

If she could live in a house made of books, she would.

She hopes you will forgive her odd sense of humour. But having fun while you learn makes you remember things better. Well, that's her excuse anyway...

Other Books By Beth

What Is Self-Esteem? How To Build Your Self-Esteem and Feel Happy Now

The Recovery Formula: An Addict's Guide To Getting Clean & Sober Forever

The Happy Addict: How To Be Happy In Recovery From Alcoholism or Drug Addiction

Forthcoming

How to Create Your Ideal Life

"Sometimes, changing just one thought, view, belief or behaviour can change your entire life."

- Me, I think.

Contents

Question Everything

Socrates was famous for a few things: sporting an astonishingly curly beard, rarely bothering with footwear, pondering, and stopping total strangers in the street to quiz them on their beliefs.

The philosopher was also famed for admitting he didn't know anything, except that he knew nothing. This doesn't bode well for a book about wisdom so far, does it?

But context is everything, as we will discover in this chapter, and acknowledging your own ignorance can pave the way to greater wisdom.

On his personal quest for insight, Socrates sought out teachers who he hoped could guide him. But he was disappointed to discover that people who claimed to be wise talked absolute waffle when he met them.

He found that while politicians might 'know' things, it didn't mean they were wise. (I'm with Socrates here; some right nit-wits get into government.) And poets have the power to create verses which move people, without there necessarily being any meaning to their words. (A bit like some of The Beatles' songs.)

After finding that people who declared themselves to be wise were actually pretty stupid, Socrates thought it better to admit what he didn't know, rather than purporting to be some brainiac.

Although many people do tend to think of Socrates as a wise man, in truth, he wasn't a guru. If he had been, he wouldn't have gone around searching for wisdom.

Socrates was a philosopher, someone whose very job description means they do not have all the answers. When his disciples called him a teacher, he refused the label, because he wasn't giving formal lessons, but trying to figure things out himself.

He did, however, come up with a very clever way for doing just that: the Socratic Method. It is basically a dialogue, where you question beliefs, hypotheses, and assumptions in order to get closer to the truth.

It is important to question everything, because we can all have faulty beliefs and innate prejudices that are so deeply entrenched that we don't even recognise that we have them. We often fall prey to cognitive biases and logical fallacies, like thinking that all taxi drivers are lunatics, just because we had one bad ride.

We make generalisations and blanket statements, and imagine that things are simply common sense, when there is often no such thing. These very human flaws make us assume that certain things must be true or false, even if they aren't. And we rarely even realise that we are basing our opinions and conclusions on false presumptions and beliefs.

For example, when hiring white-collar workers, many employers favour candidates with a degree, especially if it's from a top-class university. Often it doesn't even matter what subject the degree covers. It could be anything from Physics to Parapsychology. (Yes, you too, could become a real-life Ghostbuster – several credible unis in the US and the UK offer this course.)

Employees just assume that graduates must be more disciplined and brighter than people who didn't go to university. That is a massive leap in logic and unfair on people without a degree.

There could be any number of reasons why a genius didn't complete university. They may have had family obligations or struggled to find the time or money to go. Some may have been prevented from graduating due to unfortunate circumstances, such as ill health or suffering from a bereavement before their final exam. Research shows that many super-smart people hate formal learning. Classrooms can be very stifling and boring if your IQ is higher than the other students'.

And not everyone wants to get a degree or go to the 'best' university, even if they would be quite capable of doing so. I got good enough college grades to get into Oxford or Cambridge. My teachers were stunned that I didn't want to apply. But I hated the atmosphere of over-privilege and the silly, archaic traditions, so I was set on a less hoity-toity university in London.

After all, who wants to parade around singing about ducks or beat a load of stones with sticks on a certain date? Yes, those are genuine Oxbridge traditions that still carry on, and they don't sound very smart to me.

Using the Socratic method of questioning, here is how the philosopher might have handled someone who'd made the sweeping statement that graduates must be cleverer than non-graduates:

Socrates: "Do you not consider the invention of the electric motor, the generator, electrolysis and electro-plating to be rather clever?"

Someone: "Yes, they are amazing scientific feats."

Socrates: "Would you deem the inventor of all these things to be intelligent?"

Someone: "Well, obviously."

Socrates: "Do you think this person studied science at university?"

Someone: "For sure."

Socrates: "Have you heard of Michael Faraday?"

Someone: "He was a scientist, wasn't he? I seem to recall now that he invented some of those."

Socrates: "Did you know that Mr Faraday had no formal education at all and worked as a bookbinder?"

Someone: "No, I didn't know that. How did he come up with all that stuff then?"

Socrates: "Forgive me, but did you go to university?"

Someone: "Er, yeah, I did."

Socrates: "And what have you invented?"

Someone: "I invented a drinking game once."

Socrates: "Do you think you are smarter than Mr Faraday?"

Someone: "Look, I haven't really had time to go around inventing stuff, because I've been working at McBurgerHut. I've got a student loan to pay off, and I still owe the bar some cash for damages after that drinking game got out of hand..."

Socrates: "So, we can not assume that non-graduates are not as clever as graduates."

Someone: "OK then, so how did he come up with all that clever stuff?"

Socrates: "He read the books he was binding."

Someone: "Aha, so he was kinda taught then, even if he taught himself. We had to do a lot of reading for ourselves at uni, you know."

Socrates: "Hmm...do you know much about genes?"

Someone: "Yeah, a bit. About DNA and stuff."

Socrates: "Have you heard of Gregor Mendel, who originally discovered genetics?"

Someone: "I'm guessing he was someone else who read a lot, if he didn't go to uni."

Socrates: "No, he was a monk who liked gardening and happened to notice that his baby plants inherited certain traits from the parent plants."

Someone: "Oh."

Socrates: "Well then, we can conclude so far that some non-graduates can be just as clever as a graduate, either by self-education or having an observational mind. Let's carry on then. Have you heard of William Herschel?"

Someone: "Er, I would Socrates, but I think I'm going to be late for my shift..."

Update Your Opinions

As Socrates proved, there is nothing quite so unwise as claiming you know things to be true, when they could easily be untrue. It makes you look really daft.

If you cannot wholly prove or disprove something, you should always be open to shifting your opinion about it. Every view you hold should be up for debate if you truly want to be wise. When fresh information comes along, consider it – no matter how long you have held onto your old beliefs, nor where they first originated.

When attempting to carry out a task, have you ever been interrupted by some busybody who totally takes over while claiming in true Mr Punch fashion *"That's the way to do it!"*?

It is both frustrating, and somewhat infuriating, when someone thinks that their way of doing something is the only way that works. But people do it, fooled by familiarity and blind to other solutions (that actually might be better).

Whoever came up with the quite disturbing saying: "There is more than one way to skin a cat" was much wiser than the person who said: "The only way out is through" – and I don't care that it was super-poet Robert Frost (who did say some other, more sensible things). It just isn't true.

We can find ways around, over and across things, or we can avoid them completely. I think the idea of 'the only way' should be banished from our thoughts.

We pick up our ideologies and opinions in all sorts of ways: from our parents, teachers, politicians, friends, and the media. Often we believe something because of our own experience – without noticing how very limited our experience actually is.

I am someone who has 'lived a little', which means that I know a bit about the wilder (and harsher) side of life. But my personal knowledge is still restricted by my age, location, gender, class – and more. I have no idea what it would be like to be a homeless, old addict in China. I haven't a clue how it feels to be an agoraphobic boy raised in a Brazilian Favela.

It is only logical to admit, as Socrates did, that I don't know anything for sure, even if I have had experience of 'similar' things myself. Not acknowledging this leads to narrow-mindedness and jumping to false conclusions.

You can instantly become wiser just by opening your mind and accepting that you don't know much for certain. This attitude leaves you free to explore more possibilities and learn in a more comprehensive way.

You can use the Socratic method with others or on your own. All you have to do is question things, so that you move further away from generalisations and fallacies and nearer to the truth. The truth may be hard, multi-faceted, complex and tricky. But, life is often messy like that. Things don't always fit into a neat little box.

Lose The Labels

Be open-minded about others, too. It makes me smile when people say of behaviour that they don't expect: "That's not like him". A rigid opinion of who a person *is* can blind us to other parts of their personality.

No-one has a totally fixed character. We all have the capacity to change. And we sometimes act in different ways to adapt to various contexts.

Do you have a 'telephone voice' like I do? I talk more clearly on the phone than I do when I'm kicking back with my mates. Does that mean the 'telephone voice' is fake? No, it's just contextual. It's the same as not effing and jeffing in front of little children, while not minding your manners as much in front of friends.

Another example. You probably wouldn't walk buck-naked into a restaurant (I'm sorry if I have assumed that, and it happens to be your favourite hobby), but you may well wander about your bedroom in your birthday suit. Neither being nude nor wearing clothes are your fixed behaviours. They change, depending on what circumstances you are in.

Do you see how much context matters? Acts, words and people can vary enormously under different sets of conditions.

The same goes for groups. Just because some people in the Netherlands like to chase Edam down a hill, it doesn't make all Dutch people 'crazy cheese-rollers'. And despite what satirical cartoons may depict, I've lived with a real, live Frenchman and can confirm that he didn't wear a necklace made of onions, nor carry a baguette everywhere he went.

So, if you have made assumptions, generalisations, or held rigid views about anyone, remember that people aren't sheets of paper. They have many dimensions. By clinging fast to one opinion, you may have missed other aspects to someone's character and overlooked different qualities that they possess.

By questioning everything, we can root out our errors to help us avoid making unfair, unwise, or wrongful judgments. As we get ever closer to the truth, we are less likely to make mistakes.

But that is not the only value of the Socratic method. While at first, it may feel uncomfortable to dive into uncertainty, it is ultimately liberating. While certainty may give you a comfort blanket, sometimes that very blanket can smother you.

When you are open-minded, you are freer. You can explore exciting new ideas, find fresh solutions, and make better choices.

When your mind does not hold fast to rigid thoughts and ideologies, a type of serenity becomes available to you. And it comes in the form of equanimity.

If you are not bothered about being right and sure all the time, it is far less stressful if things turn out to be different than you originally imagined. When you are equanimous, you can brush off your errors without distress and accept new realities with ease.

The question comes to mind: "Would you rather be right or happy?" Of course, Socrates would have called out that question, as you can be both or neither.

The two states do not have to exist in opposition to one another. But for our purposes, I think you know what I mean.

By the way, I wouldn't necessarily do as Socrates did, which was stopping random strangers in the street to practice the Socratic method. You might be called a pedantic weirdo or have the police called on you for harassment. I did mention that Socrates wasn't always that wise.

But always question things in your own mind. Query what you have been told and things you have just assumed to be true.

Avoid thinking in black and white, presuming that "everyone always does X", that "all Ys are like this", or that what is true for the moment must be true and fixed forever.

Through ditching preconceptions and being open to new knowledge, you will become fairer, wiser, more flexible, and less stressed if things change.

And the very act of questioning things gives many different areas of your brain a great work-out, making you instantly smarter than you were before.

Shifty Eyes

I was once stuck in a very unhappy relationship. And who did I blame? Him, of course!

Well, he was the one going out drinking all night, coming home at all hours, and generally being daft and annoying when he did come home. No wonder I shouted at him so much.

In fact, by the time he did come home, I was so angry that I had already thought up a thousand insults, and was ready to let them fly. Once, I was screaming at him so loudly that one of our neighbours checked on us to make sure I wasn't being attacked.

And while I was still shouting, whining, and calling him names, my sozzled partner would inevitably fall asleep. It was like adding insult to injury, as if he thought that my feelings weren't worth listening to. And that would make me even angrier.

The times when I wasn't able to shake him awake to shout at him some more (I did tell you in the intro that I used to be a very unwise person), I would suffer from a sleepless night, still seething with pent-up rage and resenting every drunken snore from the other side of the bed. It was almost as if he was showing off: "Look, I'm sleeping soundly. My conscience is clear, and I'm at peace."

So then I would start kicking him or yelling: "Stop snoring!", which, of course, he was way too far gone to even hear. So my night was even further ruined by having to spend it physically assaulting my partner, rather than sleeping.

It's embarrassing to think of how badly I acted now, and to realise how utterly blind I was to what was really going on. And that was because I was only considering the situation from my own perspective.

This was back when I was trying to overcome my alcohol addiction. Not only did I hate my boyfriend's behaviour, but I thought he was selfish for going out and getting blind drunk while I was in my early days of sobriety and struggling not to cave in and drink.

I thought he must have realised how unfair it was to get completely smashed when you're going home to someone who is trying to stay sober. He must've been able to see what a triggery situation he was putting me in, not only coming home reeking and tasting of booze, but doing so when I was angry and stressed that he had been out all night.

But this also occurred at a time when I was trying to become a wiser person. And, happily, I was about to learn some things which would completely alter the way I saw the situation, how I felt about it, and how I dealt with it.

See Through Different Eyes

There is a neat little trick you can use to instantly make you feel differently about a situation. It involves changing perspectives – first by seeing through the other person's eyes, and then by observing the scene as if you were a third party.

To do this, you have to imagine physically shifting out of your own skin, and sinking into the body of the other person. In this way, you can see what they see, instead of looking at things through the lens of your preconceptions and your emotional state.

What I felt most aggrieved about during this bout of my boyfriend's behaviour was that I was sure he must know what he was doing to me, and yet he was doing it anyway. It made me feel like he didn't care about me or my feelings. But that was an assumption I had made. He had never told me any such thing.

So, I dropped my own perspective, shifted into my partner's position, and started to investigate what else might be going on. I imagined arriving home to an angry girl yelling, screaming, and calling me names.

I suddenly felt very sad. No wonder he didn't want to come home to that. No wonder he stayed out so late at night.

And I saw that he didn't understand how triggering it can be for an alcoholic in early recovery to see others drinking freely. He hadn't been to alcohol counselling as I had. He knew nothing about triggers and how they affect the addict's mind. He didn't know how the smell or taste of alcohol can cause an alcoholic to have unbearable cravings.

Through his eyes, I also saw a woman who was being very hypocritical. After all, she'd happily stayed out all night drinking before, and had not come home at all on several occasions.

And although I knew how stressed my boyfriend was at work (he had even cried in front of me, which was a very rare thing), it wasn't until I put myself in his position that I really felt the weight of that pressure and stress. I soon saw that his benders were a way of trying to cope.

I realised that, although drinking is not the ideal way to deal with stress, this man was not an alcoholic like me. However unwise his behaviour, he was allowed to let off steam by drinking if he wanted to.

I finally understood that this man was not responsible for my recovery – only I was, and I had no right telling him he couldn't drink just because I had to be sober.

By looking through my partner's eyes, I saw that I had made so many assumptions based on my own limited perspective. And I felt utterly ashamed of the way I had treated him.

After realising all that, I imagined floating out of his body and into an impartial, observational space.

I imagined that I was a stranger, looking on at these two people (me and him), and trying to make sense of what was going on.

Again, I immediately felt differently about so many things. I felt sorry for the lady who was trying to stay sober and who cared about her partner, but instead of treating him kindly, hollered at him to try and make him change.

I could see how unproductive her reactions were, and how bewildered her boyfriend was by her behaviour. He was watching her shouting, wondering what all the fuss was about and feeling even more stressed out because of her.

I saw how the two of them were trapped in a vicious cycle. He'd go out after work for a drink to relieve the day's tension. Then he would come home, only to get yelled at and face yet more stress. He then dreaded going home, and ended up staying out later and later.

Of course, this upset the lady even more. Not only was she desperately trying to stay sober, and found his behaviour triggering, but she assumed that his actions meant he didn't care about her or her efforts at sobriety. And every action she took, made them both more and more miserable.

Through the perspective of a stranger, I wondered what could be done about the problem. What would be an effective solution to end this vicious cycle and stop the suffering they were both going through?

I could only decide what the lady should do, since you can not change, or make decisions for, others. So, I concluded that she had to take responsibility for her recovery and realise that whatever her partner did, it was not a reason to relapse. And she had to see that his behaviour was not a sign that he didn't care, but a clear signal that he was stressed.

It was unwise of her to react angrily to his drinking or staying out late, because she was adding to his woes by the way she treated him when he got home.

So she had to act differently when he rolled in drunk. If his binges were due to stress, she would be better off giving him a hug or asking about his day, instead of shouting at him.

When I had come to my conclusions, I allowed myself to settle back into my own body, bringing with me all the new insights and wisdom I had gained from the other perspectives.

Putting It Into Practice

When my partner went out drinking again, I had no expectations of how drunk he would get or what time he might get back. I knew he stayed out late, and that I was probably partly to blame, because I had been so nasty to him when he got home.

So, instead of perpetually checking my watch and

boiling over with more and more rage as every hour passed, as I used to do, I entertained and distracted myself by reading one of my favourite books.

As soon as I heard the front door drunkenly slam shut, my stomach clenched with anxiety. It is hard to overcome old feelings and automatic reactions in the beginning, especially when you have followed them for so long.

So, I reminded myself that he was allowed to drink, and I wasn't, and that was the end of that. I recalled the time he cried in my lap over being so miserable at work, and my heart softened.

As soon as the bedroom door opened, I sprang out of bed and gave him a great big bear hug, the warmest cuddle I could, and asked him how his day had gone.

At first, he looked a bit taken aback – wasn't this where the shouting started? – but then he returned my hug and we stood there holding each other tightly for a long time.

"I'm glad to see you," he slurred. "I've had the most awful day at work." Then we lay down on the bed together as he told me what had happened. I stroked his head as he talked until he finally sunk into sleep.

Because I was calm now and my conscience was clear, having behaved with integrity, I fell asleep easily too, despite my partner's snoring.

That night changed everything between us. While he would still go out and get drunk, he got home earlier than he used to. And he acted more lovingly towards me in general – instead of two people at war, we became good friends again. He would confide in me, he called me his 'rock', and when he was off work, we would have fun, instead of bickering about things.

Although these were lovely changes, they weren't the most important changes of all. The most significant change happened inside me. I felt much better about myself. I was more carefree. I lost my angry edge. I felt much more peaceful. And it was because I was now doing wiser, kinder things.

When I was seething with rage and shouting at the top of my lungs, I didn't like myself. I had thought it necessary before I realised a better way of handling things. But I had been utterly miserable and hated the mouthy harridan I had become.

By looking from different perspectives, I was able to change my old behaviours and become a better, wiser person, someone who I respected much more.

In my heart, I've always had a lot of empathy, and if I ever saw anyone struggling, I would try to help them. But because my buttons were being pounded, and I was too close to the situation, I couldn't be that compassionate person who cared and wanted to help.

Taking a step back from a situation helps you to move out of the negative emotions. You can see the bigger picture, instead of being stuck in your narrow point of view, hurting inside and chasing your tail.

Looking through other people's eyes gives you instant insight and helps you find wise solutions that match your values and also get better results.

Solving Problems

You can use different perspectives to solve all sorts of problems, from personal ones to professional ones.

If you have a relationship issue, look through the other person's eyes, and then move on to the third party perspective. You may find all sorts of solutions from an impartial observer's point of view.

My 'stranger' suggested a variety of ways I could change my behaviour to get better results. I looked at them all before settling on a choice that felt right. One of the options was to talk to him calmly about the situation when he was sober, in the hope that he'd stop doing it. That might have worked, but it didn't solve the problem of his stress, so it wasn't a very fair solution for him.

Another suggestion was to plan things we could do together each night. That might have helped him de-stress, but it didn't take into account that I should be responsible for my own recovery. And it would have been impractical to do an activity five nights a week. And suppose we had done that; more than likely he would have wanted to go to a bar, or would have got drunk if we'd gone to a restaurant.

Spend a good deal of time in the third party position, so you can thoroughly review your options. The very best solution is one which is fair to all concerned, and which helps you feel at peace with yourself.

Other Tricky Issues

This technique is not limited to relationship problems. You can use it for any situation where you're feeling stuck.

Imagine you have a problem at work – not necessarily

a personal one, but just an issue you can't figure out. Look at the problem through the eyes of your boss, your colleagues, your clients – whoever is relevant – and a third party. You could even set up an imaginary board meeting and have Socrates on the panel. Have him question you on various solutions until you find one that is flawless.

You can use this technique for logistical problems too. View your plans from different angles: from the side, from below, from a bird's eye view. Zoom out to see the bigger picture and focus in to see the tiny details.

Doing this will give you fresh insights and awareness, make you more creative, help you uncover new paths, and consider things that you had never even thought to look at before.

You can even look at yourself to see all your personal resources, ones that you might have overlooked if you weren't observing yourself.

This tool can be used for practically anything, from planning a party, to writing a speech, to researching a market. You can even use it to solve jigsaw puzzles or beat your friends at chess if that's your thing.

Clearly, it is most powerful when you use it to resolve

problems that are making you or others unhappy.
Just remember that the wisest solutions will be viable,
ethical, cover all important bases, and align with your
values.

They must be as fair as humanly possible, so that you
can execute your plans with integrity, peace of mind
and self-respect.

Adventures In Wonder-land

I don't know why there is so much hostility towards our feline friends in common sayings, but curiosity hasn't killed any cats as far as I am aware.

Curiosity has killed a few people, but most of them have been people doing reckless things or were over-eager inventors, either testing out their prototypes in foolhardy ways or missing a crucial piece of data that is now common knowledge.

This explains why the number of inventors who were killed by their creations dropped sharply early in the 20th century. By that time, more was known about science and people had become more cautious about experimenting on themselves. But in former years, there were a few deaths due to experimentation and taking things a wee bit too far.

An example that springs to mind is the 'Flying Tailor', Franz Reichelt, who managed to kill himself rather carelessly in 1912. He was a tailor, obviously, but also fancied himself as an inventor. His dream was to construct a 'parachute suit'. Are you curious to know how this plan to safe-guard pilots forced to abandon their aircraft went so horribly wrong?

It was the dawn of aviation, and Reichelt was living in Paris, where he had a thriving dressmaking shop. Why couldn't he be just as successful at inventing an item which had very little to do with frills and lace and much more to do with maths and physics?

Anyway, he used his tailors' materials to start creating prototypes. First, he fixed silk wings to dummies and dropped them from the fifth floor of a block of flats. Encouraged by the fact that his mock-pilots landed safely, he attempted to incorporate the wings into a wearable suit.

But he couldn't manage to get any success with a suit. Instead of admitting that his design wasn't workable, despite being told by France's leading aeronautical organisation that it totally wasn't, Reichelt continued to develop the suit.

Now here is where benign curiosity turns into idiocy and obsession. Instead of questioning his blueprints, Reichelt blamed his failures on not having a high enough platform to effectively trial his prototype. He asked the police for permission to conduct a drop test from the Eiffel Tower.

Reichelt's final design was basically a Batman-esque

cloak with a gigantic hood. The authorities said "non" for reasons which I'm sure are blatantly obvious. But, after enduring Reichelt's repeated pestering for over a year, they finally crumbled and gave him approval.

Reichelt had assured the police that he would conduct the trial using a dummy, but when he turned up at the tower, he announced that he would test the suit on himself. When an expert aviator raised technical and safety concerns, Reichelt offered no real rebuttal. He simply boasted that his criticisms would be utterly refuted when he saw the parachute suit in action.

Despite Reichelt's friends and a crowd of spectators pleading with him not to do something so stupid, the stubborn tailor climbed the 57 metres to the tower's first platform wearing his contraption.

He jumped with a calm smile, the parachute failed to deploy, and Reichelt was killed instantly as he hit the concrete below. The end. Not for the press, though, who took the trouble to measure the depth of the dent his body had made in the pavement – 15cm, in case you were wondering.

I think we can all conclude that it was not the Flying Tailor's curiosity that killed him. Indeed, it was quite admirable, if somewhat ironic, that he was interested in inventing a safety device.

What caused Reichelt's death was his stubborn mind, his failure to question, and his limited perspective. He even used a prime example of logical fallacy when answering the aviator: i.e. dismissing a valid point with personal opinion, rather than a logical argument.

And if you read the first two chapters, you'll know the importance of all the elements Reichelt failed to cover when it comes to being wise. The Flying Tailor never stood a chance.

Sane Curiosity

Curiosity can make us wiser, as long as we approach it in the right way. You can not effectively be curious and stubborn at the same time, which is where poor old Reichelt got it so wrong.

Genuine curiosity means being inquisitive, like Alice in Wonderland. Wait, didn't Alice's curiosity get her into trouble? Not really. Her problem, again, was not listening to others, like the Cheshire Cat, who was trying to give her clues. And she ruined things by being so set on having the answers that she became frustrated and sad, when she could have just enjoyed the adventure. Yes, I know she's a fictional character, but she serves to prove a good point.

The fact that we don't necessarily get answers to all our questions doesn't matter, since the very act of flexing our curiosity muscles expands our minds. To quote Albert Einstein, "curiosity is its own reason".

So, if constantly questioning everything, as Socrates did, helps to rid us of faulty beliefs, fixed ideas and generalisations, curiosity is the natural next step. If we start wondering what the truth is, we can form new insights, outlooks and paradigms to fill in the gaps left by removing old habitual thinking.

We don't have to accept or settle on any one answer. Einstein never painted himself into a corner by calling anything he discovered a 'law'. He was happy to just consider his ideas as 'theories'. Because the moment we totally accept something, we cut off our curiosity, so the mind closes down, limiting further exploration.

But in order to be wise, we must keep the mind open, keep our brain developing, keep our sense of wonder flowing. Otherwise, we are putting limits on what is possible within our world, which is not a very smart thing to do.

By staying curious, you allow yourself to go beyond what you ever thought achievable before, keeping all possibilities open and letting you see new worlds.

The Mother Of All Invention

What would have happened if Thomas Edison had ever stopped being curious and settled for what we already knew was possible in the world? We wouldn't have electricity, the light bulb, batteries or cement, all of which he invented.

When electric lighting first came along, some people called it 'black magic', because their minds were not open enough to conceive of a day when they would ever be able to pull a cord or push a switch and have light fill the room. They were so rigidly fixed on the idea that candles were the very limit in the field of lighting, that they were probably quite shocked when gas lamps appeared, too.

You don't have to be a great inventor to be wise, but you do have to be open to innovations and be able to conceive that things that are not possible right now may one day be achieved.

You may come up with some ideas and inventions of your own if you do stay curious and keep your mind open to things that don't even exist yet or haven't been discovered. But even if you don't want to be an inventor, it is still vital to your intelligence to be able to accept and imagine that there may be other realities out there, or that in the future, everything might be completely different. Because if you don't, your mind won't stretch.

Who ever knew that you'd be able to read this book either on printed pages, rather than in my scrawly handwriting (which most of you wouldn't be able to read anyhow), or on a digital screen? Curious people, that's who.

The Curious Researchers

When you look at the evolution of society, the number of inventions, and the fresh discoveries that have been made over the years, it is self-evident that curiosity must make you smarter.

No-one would have known how to create fire without some curious caveman first staring at two sticks and wondering what might happen if they were rubbed together. And we would never have had cheese, ice-cream or milkshake if some curious soul hadn't tried pulling a cow's udder to see what would happen.

A group of curious researchers were wondering why, and how, curiosity makes us smarter. Interestingly, it was the researchers' own curiosity that drove them to carry out studies on it.

Charan Ranganath, one of the authors of the study from the University of California at Davis, wondered how curiosity might have an impact on the memory and on learning. "In any given day, we encounter a barrage of new information," the psychologist said, "but even people with really good memory will remember only a small fraction of what happened two days ago."

To research this, his team asked a group of volunteers to review over 100 random questions, such as "Who was President of the US when Uncle Sam first got a beard?" and "What does the term 'dinosaur' actually mean?" Participants then had to rate each question on how curious they were to know the actual answer.

Using an MRI scanner, the researchers monitored the participants' brain activity while they were given the questions again – this time matched with an image of an unrelated, neutral face – and then, the answers.

When it came to the questions that volunteers were most curious about, their dopamine circuits went into overdrive. Dopamine is a brain chemical that gives us a high and is released when we anticipate or receive rewards. It can motivate us to seek out things which are gratifying to the brain, such as friendship and food. And dopamine also causes cravings for more.

It seems that curiosity is like a motivational loop, first giving us a thirst for knowledge, then a buzz when we learn more about things we are curious about. And when we discover more, we may even be driven to explore that area even further.

When the researchers tested the volunteers on what they had learned later, people who had expressed a high level of curiosity about a question were more likely to remember the correct answer.

In a surprise test, volunteers were asked to recall the pictures they had seen in the scanner. Although they were shown random unremarkable faces, participants could remember the images that were paired with the questions they were most curious about. This shows that when we are in curious states, we are also able to absorb entirely unrelated information.

The scans also showed that there was more activity in the hippocampus when the volunteers were more curious. This is a brain region which is important for forming new memories. The dopamine system and the hippocampal area interacted very strongly when curiosity was heightened, making it easy for the brain to learn new things – even if some of it was not of particular interest and was unrelated to things people were actually curious about.

Study lead Matthias Gruber said: "Curiosity may put the brain in a state that allows it to learn and retain any kind of information – like a vortex that sucks in what you are motivated to learn, and also everything around it."

Clearly, curiosity is extremely powerful stuff. And you can pair it with 'boring' things that you need to remember, like when to do your tax return, in order to get stuff done. So, curiosity not only makes you smarter and more creative, but it also helps you be more productive, too.

Exercises In Curiosity

There are all sorts of ways to boost your curiosity and exercises you can do to intensify your enthusiasm for learning and help to unleash your imagination. I will give you five that you can start using right-away.

1. Think Opposite

Imagine how things would be if your current reality was totally opposite. What might it be like if you were of the opposite gender? How might life be different if trees ruled the world? What would happen if gravity didn't exist? What would the world look like if dogs kept humans as pets? If you were a horse, how might that affect your perspective?

Let yourself go a little nuts here, as I clearly have. The idea is to totally unstick you from the normal barriers in your mind and to get you to consider some really curious ideas.

2. Think of Seven Questions

Make a list of seven questions that you don't know the answer to, and would genuinely like to find out. Ponder one question very deeply every day of the week. It may be that no-one really knows the answer to these questions, but it doesn't matter. We just want to get you thinking about the possibilities. So your questions could be anything from "Why do we have nightmares?" to "Do aliens exist?"

Once you've done a question a day, make a fresh list of seven questions and the repeat the exercise again.

You may find that the things you were pondering the previous week have sparked new questions.

Repeat this exercise whenever you like, bearing in mind that the more frequently you have a 'pondering week', the better you will become at being curious, creative and imaginative.

3. Daydream

Daydreams stimulate your imagination. They connect parts of your brain that don't usually link up and can help your brain form new creative neural pathways. Don't daydream about anything dull, like what you're having for lunch later. Let your mind run wild.

You can spark off creative and curious daydreams by slightly defocussing your eyes while staring at an object and starting to see it differently. Moving your eyes upwards also works. And we all know the classic way – gaze out of a window during work.

4. The Constant Why

I'm sure if you have kids, or you've ever been a child yourself, you'll partly know this particular technique already. It kind of goes like this:

"Why can't we have a puppy, mum?"

"We haven't got room for a puppy."

"Why haven't we got room?"

"Well, we live in an apartment."

"Why do we live in an apartment?"

"Because we do."

"But why, mum?"

"Because!"

"But why?" (tugs at mum's skirt)

"That's why! Now go and do something useful like brushing your teeth or something..."

If you didn't experience this as a child or parent, I'd be extremely surprised. But we can use this normally frustrating discourse to become wiser.

In this exercise you're going to be the child and the mother, but you're going to ask questions until you get a satisfactory answer.

Don't cut yourself off with a "Because!" or "That's why!" Ask the question "why?" until you can literally ask it no more.

Choose questions that are interesting or challenging, such as: "Why do some people choose to smoke?" or "How did Donald Trump get elected?" Dig down deeper into the issues with more and more 'whys' until you can either realistically answer your question or you come to an impasse. If you ever find out the answer to the second question, let me know.

5. Dream Up Ways to Pique Your Curiosity

No, this isn't a cop-out because I couldn't think of a fifth task. It's the ultimate exercise in curiosity. If you can create tools and techniques you can use to spark your own curiosity, you will be actively using your curiosity muscle as well as figuring out what works well for you.

Ask yourself some questions like: "What makes me tick?", "What truly inspires me?", "When do I feel at my most curious?" and "What motivates me to ask questions?"

Enjoy being curious about your own curiosity!

Sportacus

Humans were designed to exercise. That's why we have so many joints, muscles and balance centres. Sloths clearly weren't designed to exercise, nor tortoises. But as humans, the ability and need to exercise is built into our very DNA.

Some people love a good jog around the park (not me) or hitting the gym (nuh-uh), while others prefer to eat right so they don't get flabby and fat. (I'd rather sacrifice cake than have to sweat in front of strangers.)

Doing exercise instantly makes you smarter. And the great news is, no matter what exercise you like, doing it will give you an immediate mental boost, because any exercise that gets your heart pumping does. I will explain exactly why this is shortly.

But first, I wanted to deliver the even more fabulous news that there is a super-sneaky way to benefit from "exercise smarts" for those who detest the thought of a treadmill, a burpee or wearing Lycra. Yay!

OK, enough celebrating. Let's move onto the science. The reason why exercise will give you an instant hit of intelligence is because it sends oxygen to the brain.

When you have more oxygen in your brain, it's easier to think, learn, and do all sorts of cool cognitive tasks, such as decision-making, remembering information and solving problems. I won't make a joke here about 'jogging your brain', as tempting as it is.

Studies have shown that people are significantly more productive on days when they exercise than they are on days when they don't. And exercisers outperform people who don't exercise on tricky cognitive tasks. And as I said, this goes for any aerobic exercise, from Taekwon-Do to table-tennis.

If you're not very keen on getting sweaty, you will be pleased to know that even walking raises the levels of oxygen in your brain. And walking has some other brilliant cognitive benefits, as we'll see shortly. Don't forget that dancing, hula-hooping and sex all count as exercise too – if you're doing it vigorously enough. So, whatever exercise you're doing, if you enjoy it and it's doing you good, keep doing it.

However, if you are prepared to try out something new, there are certain types and modes of exercising that can make us smarter in quite specific ways. So, if you want to boost a particular part of your brain, you can – just by changing your work-out.

Super Sports

Let's start off with a nice, gentle stroll. Many of us intuitively go for a walk if we've got a tricky problem to solve and can't seem to arrive at an answer. And science shows us why we do it. People who walked for 45 minutes three times a week outperformed non-walkers on a focused-attention task in a study by the University of Illinois at Urbana-Champaign.

Walkers were able to filter out distractions and focus on the task at hand. And the parts of the brain that activated showed that they were not even struggling or forcing themselves to focus. The activity was more or less effortless. You can increase your concentration even further if you walk in a natural environment, rather than an urban one. A 2008 study done by the University of Michigan revealed that interacting with nature had a similar effect on people's ability to avoid distractions.

Yoga can also sharpen your focus and has the added benefits of improving speed and accuracy on working memory tests, according to a study published in 2013. Students beat their own scores on cognitive tests after performing one 20-minute session of Hatha yoga, as compared to when they had spent 20 minutes jogging on a treadmill.

What gave them the edge after practising yoga? Study lead, Neha Gothe, explained that yoga comprises of regulated breathing and meditation, in addition to physical movements. "The practice involves an active attentional or mindfulness component," she said. The extra elements calm and focus the mind, as well as increasing self-awareness.

Do gymnastics if you want to improve your visual-spatial cognition. People with enhanced visual-spatial skills are ace at understanding and fixing equipment, problem-solving, learning academically, navigating, calculating, and estimating distances. Essentially, they make great surgeons, IT bods, architects, and pilots. I'd imagine they are pretty hot at parallel parking too.

A 2013 study carried out at Regensburg University compared the visual-spatial skills of football players, gymnasts and non-athletes by using a mental rotation task. This test involves matching an object which has spun around from its original position with the same item in a new position. The gymnasts performed best.

Other studies show that golf and combat sports, such as fencing and karate, can also improve visual-spatial skills. Hi-yah! And if you ever wondered why Bruce

Lee made those funny noises, it's because it ensures you're breathing properly and focuses your energy.

I mentioned some animals which weren't designed to exercise earlier on, but research on rats and mice show that rodents clearly are. Studies on rodents are often conducted in place of humans when researchers want to ensure that every variable is fully accounted for. (i.e. You don't have to take into account whether a mouse is rich or poor, smokes, drinks, particularly likes knitting, or anything else that varies in humans and can influence a test.)

In a 2006 review, published by The Beckman Institute, researchers revealed that mice got smarter by simply running on a wheel. Running helped the rodents with spatial learning, with some creatures managing a 12-fold increase in performance after exercise.

Running rodents also had more newborn neurons in their brains than sedentary controls. Exercise boosted mice's working memories and improved the plasticity of their brains, too.

Some researchers *do* trust humans not to mess up testing, and they explored running even further using real volunteers. If you want to become a walking dictionary, sprinting might be your exercise of choice.

In a study published in *Neurobiology of Learning and Memory*, people were able to learn words 20 per cent faster after they had performed high-impact sprints than they could after low-impact running.

Why Does Exercise Make Us Brainy?

Aside from the oxygen boost to the brain, there is an additional reason why work-outs make us smarter.

Exercise significantly raises levels of a special protein called Brain Derived Neurotrophic Factor (BDNF) in the hippocampus. BDNF regulates neurotransmitters, helping us attain a healthy balance of brain chemicals. It helps your neurons to thrive and encourages your brain to grow new ones.

But, most crucially, BDNF helps your brain make new neuronal connections, which reinforces learning and enhances brain-power. Going back to The Beckman Institute's review, researchers found that the boost in BDNF produced by exercise enhanced many cognitive processes, but the largest effect of all was on executive control functions. These include the ability to plan, to use your memory in an effective way, and to multi-task.

The review also revealed that adding strength and

flexibility training to aerobic exercise produced even more mental agility. As we have seen, certain sports have specific ways of making you smarter, so mixing it up could help you get better at all sorts of cognitive tasks.

But I Hate Exercise!

I promised the people who despise anything remotely sporty a trick to benefit from 'exercise smarts'. And I haven't forgotten. I have left it until last because it is just so mind-blowing.

The sneaky secret is that you don't even have to do any exercise to benefit from its cognitive effects – you just have to imagine you're doing it. Pretty amazing, huh? I'm imagining myself doing a happy dance right now.

Ohio's Cleveland Clinic Foundation did a really cool experiment in 2004. They got one group of volunteers to physically flex a muscle on a regular basis over 12 weeks, and another group to just imagine flexing that same muscle for the same period of time. And there was a control group which did nothing.

Obviously, the group who actually flexed the muscle saw gains in strength and a boost to their brainpower.

But, so did the volunteers who only imagined moving the muscle! The control group did not benefit in any significant way.

The results were the same whether the participants were asked to flex, or imagine flexing, either a finger or an elbow. And they only had to do their 'exercise' for five minutes a day, five times a week.

The Cleveland Clinic Foundation then tried their luck with a larger muscle – the bicep – and even recorded the electrical activity in the volunteers' brains and arms to ensure that they weren't actually moving, but were only imagining doing it.

But no-one was cheating. The results were the same again – mental exercise created larger muscles and more brainpower without the participants doing anything physical at all.

And these sorts of results have been replicated by more researchers. In 2007, a Canadian study proved that the same thing was possible when weightlifting students used only their imagination to exercise their hip muscles.

So, how on Earth is this possible?, you're probably wondering. Or maybe you're not. Perhaps you're now imagining doing 100 effortless sit-ups to achieve a perfectly-toned tum.

Well, the researchers' explanations for this amazing phenomenon was that the brain was sending signals to the motor neurons in the muscles, causing them to grow, and that the brain gains were caused by the participants' intense focus on the imaginary exercise, causing more activity in the pre-frontal cortex, which plays a role in many complex cognitive processes.

I'll put it in a shorter, slightly less sciencey way for you. The brain often has a hard time telling reality from non-reality and can activate accordingly.

Have you ever woken up from a nightmare and still felt shaky for a while, even though you're awake and safely tucked in bed? The dream seemed so real, that even though you've become conscious that it didn't really happen, your brain and your body take some time to catch up.

Have you ever recalled an embarrassing experience, and felt the same mortification all over again? Or have you ever fondly remembered a holiday and felt happier just thinking about it, even though you're nowhere near the beach, and are actually sat at your desk or doing the dishes?

The mind is both super-powerful and easily-fooled, which seems contradictory. But this odd paradox can work to our advantage in some wonderful ways. If you imagine you can achieve something, then you can, including a flat belly or toned abs, even if you never leave the comfort of your couch.

And it doesn't just work with physical exercise. Your potential is practically limitless if you use the paradox wisely.

There is much more on this in the second book in the Wiseism series, *How to Create Your Ideal Life*. But we will also cover some more cool stuff that exploits this mechanism later on in this very book.

Keep Calm And Carry On

Now, pinching the tail of a rat isn't very nice, is it? Especially if the poor creature hasn't done anything to you.

But scientists will be scientists, and in the name of research, that is exactly what some uni professors did to prove a point about stress and performance. I'll go into the exact details of the study later. But for now let's keep calm and carry on with a secret about what can instantly make you smarter.

Most people assume that pressure makes us perform better at tasks. When high stakes are involved, surely we're going to do our very best to succeed, aren't we?

We've probably all watched nail-biting matches in the world of sport, where one team or player looks totally down and out, only to rally and defeat the opposition.

Sorry to be self-indulgent, but I have to mention UK footie team Manchester United's stunning comeback against the German team Bayern Munich in the 1999 Champions League final to give you an example of this. Yes, I do absolutely have to. Read on to see why.

Manchester United were already under pressure to complete 'the treble', having won both the Premier League and the FA Cup that season.

But just six minutes into the match, Bayern scored, courtesy of Mario Basler. With plenty of time left to play, United tried to score, but Bayern's defence was well-organised and closed United down at every turn.

Growing in confidence, Bayern looked increasingly dangerous on the counter-attack. As the clock ticked down, the German team looked even stronger and United looked like they would never score.

Ninety minutes was up, the Bayern fans were setting off celebratory flares, and my boyfriend had already texted me a consolatory message.

Only three minutes of injury time was added to the match, announced just as United had won a corner. They looked desperate, and even their goalie came up to add numbers to the penalty area.

After the ball pinged to and fro between the players, Teddy Sheringham managed to hit the back of the net, 36 seconds into injury time.

At 1-1, it looked like United had forced the game into

extra time. But with just 43 seconds of injury time left to play, Ole Gunnar Solskjaer fired into Bayern's goal, giving United the lead.

As the game restarted, the referee had to drag many of Bayern's players off the ground to carry on. They were dumbstruck and despairing, having believed just minutes before that the title was theirs. Even the match officials had tied Bayern Munich ribbons to the trophy, ready to present it to the team.

Eventually, the final whistle blew – and that, as they say, is history. Man United had completed the treble and I had no fingernails left at all.

I have either made you very bored or slightly stupid by telling you that tension-filled story. It depends on whether you're a football fan or not.

If you are into football, then, love or loathe United, you will have that game etched in your memory for all time. Man U's comeback was utterly formidable – but here's the kicker. This is not the norm when it comes to performance.

No, what United achieved was extremely special. We always remember when someone makes an amazing comeback against all odds – precisely because it is so rare. Contrary to popular belief, when you are under pressure, you are not more likely to perform better. In fact, you are much more likely to make mistakes and totally mess things up.

For every time a sports star or a team has made a brilliant comeback under intense pressure, there will be a thousand more times when they totally choked.

It is calmness and composure that makes us wiser, not pressure. You actually become smarter when you are relaxed and mellow – and being calm gives you lots of cognitive benefits.

Help! I'm About To Be Eaten By A Tiger!

You don't have to fear for my safety – there is no actual tiger in the room.

But if there was, I'd probably be having all sorts of stupid thoughts right now.

Maybe I should jump out of the window to escape (well, if the tiger didn't kill me, a drop from the third floor probably would); perhaps I could just throw it a bit of chicken (I don't have any chicken with me); maybe I could make friends with it (I'm not sure that we share the same interests – I'm into football, while he looks like he's more into eating people); maybe I could hide behind a lamp (I've clearly watched too many Tom and Jerry cartoons for my own good).

Actually if there were a tiger, I'd probably attempt to run away. But the figurative tiger is an example of modern stress, which we react to in the same way as if there were a real tiger about to pounce on us.

Our response goes back to ye olden days, when we lived in caves and had a host of predators to fear. Our brains and bodies haven't yet caught up with the fact that we don't nowadays, and it treats bosses, board meetings, dating and crucial football matches as if they were all tigers.

As part of our old survival mechanisms, when we encounter something stressful, our parasympathetic nervous system (PNS) shuts down. This leaves our sympathetic nervous system (SNS) free to go into over-drive.

When the SNS takes over, our muscles tense up, our heart races and our breathing speeds up, ready to run away from that tiger. Well, that's great. We'll be safe.

But crucially, all functions that are not critical to our immediate survival in the face of a threat shut down –

and that includes the ability to think clearly to make good decisions.

When the SNS is in charge, we are more likely to be impulsive or rigid in our thoughts. We lose the ability to mull things over properly or think about long-term consequences. Creativity goes out of the window, as we are focused only on mere survival.

Now you know why people lost in the Grand Canyon or stuck in the middle of a jungle make some really daft decisions on the TV show *The Day I Almost Died*.

So, what else goes on in the body when we're under stress? The brain floods with dopamine, making us dopey, forgetful, prone to black-and-white thinking, and less able to plan or analyse.

Hang on a minute. Didn't I say dopamine was a good thing earlier? Brain chemicals are complex things and how they interact with each other and different brain areas is crucial to the response they cause in us.

Let's return to those poor rats, whose tails were being pinched, to explain this more thoroughly.

So those mean scientists at the University of British Columbia wanted to find out why dopamine had this mind-numbing effect when stress was present, but *not* when we are doing something rewarding, such as winning at Monopoly or eating dessert.

When a living creature is stressed, it produces more glucocorticoids – a particular type of hormone. In humans, the main one is cortisol, also known as 'the stress hormone'.

So, the researchers pinched the tails of rats to make them feel stressed – and sure enough, they released more dopamine into the brain. But when they blocked glucocorticoid receptors, the rats didn't release any dopamine in response to the pinch. The first clue.

The researchers then tried to discover which regions of the brain interacted with the dopamine to produce cognitive impairments. They discovered that stress produced an overload of dopamine in the pre-frontal cortex, switching it off. As we have seen already, this brain area is responsible for reasoning, working memory and a whole host of important cognitive functions.

So, what the poor rats taught researchers was that the mind-melt produced by acute stress was a result of an interaction of glucocorticoids and dopamine in the pre-frontal cortex. And that's why we become stupid under pressure, but not while eating a doughnut or beating our friends at board games.

Stress also affects our emotional intelligence, which is where true wisdom lies. You can have the highest IQ in the world, but you'll never be really wise unless you are able to use your intuition, connect with other people, and empathise as well. Stress blocks the positive feelings that help engender emotional intelligence. And, no, they didn't find that out from rats.

Feeling Over-Emotional?

It is not just stress and pressure that make us stupid. Any time we are in a highly emotional state, we are likely to become a bit dumber.

Ever been in a massive argument and said something you regret later? Ever gone all gooey over someone and been completely tongue-tied in their presence? Ever met a celebrity and said something totally inane to them? (I've done this – and, no, I'm not telling you who it was or what I said. It's way too embarrassing.) Anger, love and excitement can all cause an acute case of 'the stupids'.

As we noted in the last chapter, the brain can't always

tell the difference between what is real and what isn't, so even imagined things that put us in states of high emotional arousal can cause us to become a bit daft.

This is why when we start worrying about things that haven't even happened, we become highly irrational. This can create a vicious cycle, as our imagination runs away with us, creating increasingly awful, and highly unlikely, scenarios.

One of the worst things about all of this is that once your 'stupidity' has been turned on, it can take a long time for it to turn off. It may be hours before we stop being mindless fools.

We clearly want to avoid angry, stressed and fearful states, but there's nothing wrong with being in love or getting excited about something. So, the key to not losing your mind when you're over the moon is learning how to calm down when you need to, which is what we will cover next.

Since this is a book about becoming smarter, I will teach you some chilling-out methods that have brain benefits in addition to the relaxation factor. Another important thing to know is how to turn your SNS off. This will automatically switch your PNS back on and get your brain back online. We'll be covering how to do that too, so you don't have to be a total donkey for hours after randomly bumping into Robert De Niro.

How To Keep Calm

1. Have a Cuppa

Simple yet effective, and the secret weapon employed by British grannies to chill other people out. Tea is so soothing it can cut stress levels in half, science has shown. Tea also has the amazing ability to make you feel relaxed and alert at the same time.

Black and green tea contain caffeine, known to wake up the brain. Research by Coimbra University found that lacing mice's drinking water with caffeine made them calmer when they were subjected to stress. Nice to see scientists being kind to rodents for once.

Both varieties of tea also contain Theanine, which stimulates alpha brainwaves and creates the chemical GABA in the brain. This mixture is responsible for the feeling of tranquillity and simultaneous mental clarity we get from tea. Theanine can also aid learning and focus, since it boosts dopamine levels too.

Some herbal teas are also very calming, although they won't all give you an extra brain boost. Chamomile, valerian, peppermint, passionflower, lemon balm, and rose tea are all worth trying if you just want to relax, while green tea is the best for creating a calm, yet alert state of mind.

2. Get Grounded

Getting yourself grounded is the number one way of switching your PNS back on and shutting your SNS down, so you can stop being a blithering idiot and access your higher cognitive functions once more.

As I mentioned before, the effects of SNS activation can linger and even form a loop, where you are stuck in the stress, possibly replaying things in your head that have made you angry or afraid, which just causes you to freak out even more.

So, what you need to do is bring yourself back into the present moment as soon as you can, and here are some ways of doing that:

- Be Mindful of Your Body

Bring your attention to your bodily sensations, which are happening here and now. Focus on the feeling of your feet on the floor or the sensation of your socks or shoes against the soles of your feet. You can even rub your feet together to create a new physical sensation to anchor you in the present moment.

- Belly-breathe

Inhale through your nose, allowing your breath to fill your lungs until you feel your diaphragm move down (your belly should push out at this point). Hold the breath for a few seconds, then exhale slowly through your mouth (your diaphragm should rise up, making your belly flat again). Repeat until you are calm.

- Count With Your Senses

Count five things you can see in your immediate environment, then five things you can hear, then five things you can feel or touch. Also notice what you can smell or taste. Repeat the cycle until you're relaxed.

- Relax Your Muscles

Relaxing your muscles sends a signal to your brain, reassuring it that there is no threat nor tiger. There are various ways of doing this, such as getting a massage, taking a bath, or doing progressive muscle relaxation exercises.

3. Do Gentle 'Energy' Exercises

Tai Chi, Yoga and Qi Gong are gentle exercises which aim to direct energy to different places in or around the body – and they can all activate the PNS. These relaxing exercises also have proven cognitive benefits. We've already seen what Hatha yoga can do, so what about the others?

Sydney University carried out an experiment with cancer patients who were suffering from impaired cognitive function, either due to the disease itself or the side effects of medication. Half the patients practised Qi Gong for 10 weeks. A control group just received their normal treatment. The cancer sufferers who had done weekly Qi Gong reported substantially increased cognitive ability compared to the control group.

A review of past Tai Chi research by the University of Georgia in 2013 concluded that doing Tai Chi had positive effects on overall cognitive functioning, with a profound impact on verbal working memory. So if you're always forgetting to pick up the groceries your other half asked you to collect, get into Tai Chi and astound them when you don't forget a single item.

4. Shut off Stimulation

Not only does excessive stimulation induce stress, but it also inhibits your creativity and your ability to learn new things.

A study carried out by the University of California at Irvine showed that people who had constant access to email had higher heart rates than those who were not being bombarded with messages all day long.

More research on rats showed that, while the rodents created new neurons when experiencing something new, it was only when they had down-time that those neurons moved from the hippocampus into the rest of the brain, storing what they had learned in their long-term memory. I'm wondering now how exactly rats kick back and chill.

Anyway, this shows why you should always take study breaks, so your brain can cement your learning. Plus, you can have a nice cuppa at the same time.

Besides shutting off your electronic devices for a bit, there many other ways to cut down on stimulation. Anything which moves your focus to a less 'busy' and frantic environment will work.

Being in the countryside or by the sea cuts visual and

aural stimulation significantly. Instead of neon lights, street arguments, loud neighbours and car horns, you will only hear birds tweeting in the trees or the gentle ripple of waves. Plus, you'll be mostly surrounded by greenery or bluery, giving your brain a nice rest.

When you can instantly relax and shift into your PNS, you'll always be able to function at a higher mental level, giving you an immediate cognitive advantage.

We can take this even further and show how less external stimulation leads to a clearer head and the ability to focus on developing even more profound mental skills and emotional intelligence.

You might think that living in the forest or a cave with little to eat and no bed to sleep on, you'd get a little cranky. Add to that, a limited range of pastimes, most of which involve sitting still and silent for hours. It sounds like a boring and harsh way of life. But Buddhist monks do this and they are some of the most serene, happy and wise people in the world.

Living with less stimulation really does make you calmer and gives you the chance to focus on your mental development. There are very few distractions in a cave, after all.

In the Thai Forest tradition of Buddhism, for example, spending time in quiet solitude is a vital part of the practice. You can't self-reflect and hone your mind nearly as well when your phone is beeping, the TV is blaring, and the neighbours are having their third row of the day about whose turn it is to do the dishes.

If you don't fancy becoming a monk or nun and can't get away from it all, then take a mental break instead – focused meditation, taking a nap, dimming the lights, having a shower, or simply closing your eyes give your brain less 'work' to do, helping it to relax, rejuvenate and be more insightful.

So this should be something you should stop and do on a daily basis, even if you haven't noticed your stress levels building up – we often miss the signs and only see it when we've already snapped.

You will never be able to develop advanced levels of wisdom unless you make time for peace and quiet. Even if you can only take short breaks away from stimulation for 10 minutes at a time, you will still benefit from being calmer and better able to tap into higher cognitive functioning. The effect of these calm and quiet moments will spill over positively into the rest of your day.

Be Childlike

I said "childlike", not "childish". There will be no temper tantrums or spilled orange squash in this chapter, thank you very much.

In some ways, kids can be much cleverer than adults. Children are naturally inlined to adventure, imagine, experiment, explore, and look at things from different angles. It's how they learn about the world.

As we noted in the "but, why..?" exercise, children are inquisitive and thirsty for knowledge and reasons. They try to get to the roots of problems and actively attempt to overcome obstacles. Children can be very persistent, while adults often give up too easily if they can't seem to figure something out. Adults can also be guilty of accepting and assuming too much and find it hard to break free from their fixed ideas.

Grown-ups usually use their past experiences to solve problems, making it hard to approach issues from a fresh perspective or find creative solutions. But in some situations, it may be much smarter to consider alternative ideas, especially if you're stuck on a tricky problem and can't solve it in your usual way.

Kids' lack of experience and knowledge, on the other hand, can be an advantage. It means they are open to many possibilities, and not limited to one point of view. They try out new things more readily.

All of these qualities can mean that thinking like a child sometimes can make you wiser.

If you can learn to switch between the perspective of a child and that of an adult, looking at issues through both enquiring and educated eyes, you can access more resources, making you instantly smarter.

Riddle Me This

Children are often better at solving riddles and logic problems than adults.

There are some types of puzzle that baffle adults and yet children can solve them with ease. I'll explain why that is later, but first let's test you out by giving a few brainteasers a go.

1. The Car Park Problem

You have 20 seconds to solve the puzzle after you have read the question.

Q: What is the number of the parking space in which the car is parked?

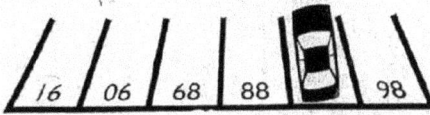

Tick, tick, tick. OK, your time is up. Did you get it?

A six-year-old can usually solve this problem in just seconds. In fact, the test comes from an entry exam to a Hong Kong primary school. Not to rub it in, if it did have you stumped.

Did you do any mathematical equations, think about your times-tables, or try to work out if there was a complex pattern? That is what most adults will do. But if you did, you were wasting your time.

Most six-year-olds will be able to tell you that the answer is clearly 87. You can see why, by simply turning the image upside-down. The numbers are, in fact, in sequence, running from 86 to 90.

2. Stuck In The Bathroom

You're in a bathroom with no windows. There is no way in or out of the room, except through a single door. You're quite into minimalism, so there are only the essentials in the bathroom. You decide to have a bath, so you turn on the taps and shut the bathroom door. But as you do, the handle snaps, so now you can't open the door. You then turn off the taps, but one of the knobs breaks, so the water keeps flowing. No-one else is in the house, so you can't call for help.

The question is: How do you save yourself from drowning?

If you've spent more than five minutes trying to figure this out, then I'm going to put you out of your misery.

The answer is that you pull the plug out of the bath. Again, a child is likely to guess this more quickly than an adult.

3. Guess The Number

OK here's another one. I will just warn you that your average three-year-old can solve this within five to 10 minutes.

If you are a computer programmer, you have a little bit of an edge, as they can generally guess the number in an hour, although that's not quite as impressive as the matter of minutes it would take a toddler.

The rest of us mere mortals may struggle. But have a go anyway. If possible, find an IT guy or gal to help you. Or even better, find a small child.

8809 = 6	7111 = 0	2170 = 1	6666 = 4
1111 = 0	3213 = 0	7662 = 2	9313 = 1
0000 = 4	2222 = 0	3333 = 0	5555 = 0
8193 = 3	8096 = 5	1012 = 1	7777 = 0
9996 = 4	7756 = 1	6855 = 3	9881 = 5
5531 = 0	2581 = ?		

Did you get it? If not, don't worry. It doesn't mean you are a dullard. Most adults struggle with this one and eventually give up.

The answer is actually 'two'. But I'll bet you still don't know why that is. The key to answer, again, lies not in complex mathematics, but in looking at the shapes of the numbers.

Count the number of loops in each series of numbers. The number 2581 has two loops in the eight, and none in any of the other digits, making the answer 'two'.
Go back and check all the numbers and you'll see the answers are all based on the number of circles in the shapes.

Some people claim to get the answer 'two' as well, by doing weird things with number substitution. Even if you could solve it that way (I don't see how, but then, I'm rubbish at maths), it would take you much longer than simply counting the loops, which is how little kids do it.

4. Which Way Is The Bus Driving?

Next, a puzzle courtesy of the National Geographic Channel. You must guess which direction the bus is travelling in. I'll just pre-warn you that 80 per cent of children aged 10 or under solved this one instantly, while most adults were completely stumped by it.

Here is the bus:

There appear to be no clues in the picture, do there? I'll give you one – the correct answer will depend on the country you live in.

What do you mean that hasn't helped?

OK, the answer: If you live in a country that drives on the right side of the road (such as the US), the bus is travelling left. If you normally drive on the left-hand side of the road (like in the UK), then your answer should be that the bus is headed right.

But how is it possible to know that when both ends of the bus look exactly the same? I gave you a clue when I said there were no clues in the picture.

You figure out the answer by what you can't see – the bus doors. Since they aren't visible, then they must be on the other side of the bus. Bus doors are always placed on the side closest to the pavement, so people can board safely.

How Do Kids Solve These Puzzles?

So why could children solve these head-scratchers, while adults struggled with them?

With the car park puzzle, children's tendency to look at things from a variety of angles helps them to work out the solution fast. Adults tend to be rigid in their point of view – unless they've studied the previous chapters and have already learned not to be.

Adults also overthink things in a way that kids just don't. Most adults look at the numbers and assume it must be a complicated maths problem, while children look for simple solutions first.

It's a similar case with the bathroom puzzle. Adults look at the limitations, which are really just red herrings, as there is a simple solution in just pulling out the plug. But adults will overlook that, thinking there must be some super-tricky answer to work out.

Overcomplicating matters doesn't always help us, especially when there is a simple answer rooted in common sense.

I'll give you an example of this from my childhood. My very first goal in life was to become a princess. I was about four since you ask, and, no, it's no longer one of my dreams.

Anyway, I told my mother that's what I wanted to be when I grew up and I was utterly flabbergasted when she asked me how I was going to manage that. The answer was so simple. "I'll marry a prince, of course," I said.

Now, you may laugh (as my mother did), but I'm from England, which is a pretty small island. And we actually have one prince who is almost the same age as me – William. He even shares my birthday, albeit he is two years younger than I am.

He eventually married Kate Middleton, but if I had been dogged enough in my pursuit of marrying a prince, I could have taken her place. As all good gold-diggers know, you can hang out in the same places that celebrities do to increase your chances of bagging a star boyfriend.

It would have been surprisingly easy to get access to Prince William. He met Kate Middleton in the halls of the university they both attended – St. Andrews. I was accepted into UCL, which is harder to get into than St. Andrews, so I would have been able to go to the same university as the prince if I had wanted to. Then, it would been a question of using my charm.

And even if Prince William hadn't taken a shine to me, there was also Prince Harry, only four years my junior, and he probably would have liked me more than his older bother would have. Harry was well-known as a wild-child and was often spotted falling out of London night-clubs. I was living in London at the time. If you read the introduction to this book, you'll know that I was an utter alkie, so we probably would have got on pretty well.

Newspapers often mentioned which particular clubs Harry went to. So, if I had tarted myself up and gone to those nightspots, instead of hanging out in my local, it would have been possible to bump into the prince. None of his girlfriends have been particularly posh, so I would have been at no disadvantage there.

See, ma? My answer wasn't so stupid. If I had wanted to pursue that dream, looking through the eyes of both a child and an adult might have got me there. Picking simple solutions and believing that anything is possible, like a child, and then exploiting an adult perspective to plan and strategise might have made me a royal after all.

Anyway, back to the puzzles. There are two main reasons why children can "guess the number" in the series more easily than adults.

The first comes from that overthinking muscle that adults like to exercise so much. But the second is due to how children view the world – and this is what helps with the bus brainteaser too. Children literally see the world differently from adults. Adults tend to take a picture as a whole, while children are able to break images down into single elements more easily.

In fact, until around the age of 12, children literally *cannot* visually process information in the same way as adults by taking multiple cues and putting them together. They have to separate out what they see.

Research carried out by UCL and Birkbeck in 2004 showed that adults blend different visual cues, such as texture, depth and information from different eyes (binocular vision) to make a unified image, whereas children separate different visual data.

But adults' ability to integrate different varieties of sensory information comes with a price known as 'sensory fusion'. Once the information has become combined, adults will lose the knack of being able to separate it out again. This means that they can't easily make sense of conflicting visual cues.

Ever been fooled by an optical illusion? And been totally unable to see beyond what your brain is telling you must be the case? That's sensory fusion.

In one experiment, volunteers had to guess which of two objects was the most slanted. When perspective and binocular information conflicted, six-year-olds outperformed adults. The kids were able to spot the differences by separating the visual cues.

The test was akin to placing a large monster truck in the distance, and a tiny, matchbox one, painted to blur out its details, nearby. This confuddles adults' brains. They expect to be able to see more detail in close-up objects and faraway items to be fuzzier. Adults also expect the same object to look larger when it's closer. So they'd probably assume that the matchbox truck was further away. Kids would not make that mistake.

This explains why, when looking at the picture of the bus, most adults were not able to see past the fact that the vehicle looked the same from both ends. A child, however, would be far less concerned with the confusing information, and therefore more likely to notice what was missing in the image – the bus doors.

It also helps to explain why kids could "guess the number" more quickly than most adults. They could see no clear code in the numbers, so they switched to a simpler mechanism instead: looking at shapes.

So, next time you have what seems like a complex problem, think and see like a child. Break the issue down, look for simple solutions first, and don't make things more complicated than they actually may be.

Children Are Creative

Just give a child a box and see what they can do with it. To you, it might just be a boring old box for storing or packing things. For kids, it can be a bus, a cave, a castle, or anything else that they want it to be.

Children are so imaginative that they can play with a simple object for hours without ever tiring of it, as they make up new worlds or roles to exist in.

Did you ever have an imaginary friend as a child? If so, don't think that you are some kind of loser.

Research done by the Universities of Washington and Oregon revealed that 65 per cent of children will have had an invisible friend by the age of seven. It's a very creative way to escape boredom and is more popular among only or elder children, who are less likely to have an accessible playmate.

Kids are very inventive, too. I know loads of people, and the only person I know who has ever invented anything is an eight-year-old named Toby. With no special training, and using only a cheap science kit he got for Christmas, my friend's little nephew managed to invent a 'static-o-meter'.

Noticing that his hair went all fuzzy after bouncing on the trampoline in his back garden, Toby wanted to figure out how much static was generated based on the length of time he bounced. We've all wondered that, haven't we? No? Time to start trampolining then. You already know the exercise will make you smarter, and you can bounce while doing a curiosity exercise.

Anyway, Toby *was* curious about it, so he got a test-tube, some chemicals, and goodness knows what else (I don't even know how the thing worked and I got a double-A* in my Science GCSEs), and he created a tool which could measure static electricity.

We tried it out, and sure enough, the chemicals in the test-tube shot up to varying levels depending on how long we bounced for.

But why on Earth did he invent such a thing and how did he do it? It comes down to the natural curiosity that children have and their creative ways of solving problems. And now Toby knows precisely how long he can use his trampoline for without messing up his hair before school.

I don't know if Toby invented something totally new.

The Van de Graaff machine and semi-conductors are the only things I am aware of which measure static electricity. But both of those things are much more complex than sticking some chemicals in a tube. Toby chose a simpler solution.

And if it hasn't been officially invented yet, the kid should patent the static-o-meter. It would be much easier and cheaper to produce than the current tools we use to check static levels.

He'd also earn himself a place in the record books as one of the youngest inventors of all time.

But Toby wouldn't be the very youngest. That title is thought to belong to a five-year-old boy, who came up with his invention when he was only three years of age, receiving a patent for it when he was five.

Sam Broughton, a British toddler, was watching his father sweeping the yard and noticed that he kept changing brooms. Curious, he asked his dad why he kept swapping brushes. Mr Broughton told Sam that he had to use a large broom to collect up all the leaves and twigs and swapped to a smaller one to sweep up little items, such as dirt and dust.

So Sam ran to the shed, grabbed a large elastic band,

and connected the two brooms so they could work in tandem. He fixed the coarser brush in front to pick up the bigger objects and the finer one at the back to pick up smaller debris left behind. Ta-da! He had invented the double-headed broom.

Again, it was a simple idea sparked by curiosity, the will to find solutions, and a child's less complicated way of seeing the world. When asked if he wanted to be an inventor when he grew up, Sam said he didn't know, but had found the experience fun.

Several kids have come up with some pretty cool inventions, all in the name of fun. A 12-year-old boy named Peter Chilvers invented windsurfing when he attached a sail to his surfboard. And our friend Toby would have approved of 16-year-old George Nissen, who invented the first modern trampoline.

Horatio Adams invented chewing gum when he was in his mid-teens. His father was trying to create a rubber substitute, but young Horatio realised that the substance his dad was using, Mexican Chicle, was chewable. So, he created 200 gumballs and asked the neighbourhood drugstore to sell them. When he went to check on sales at mid-afternoon, the gumballs had already sold out.

And an 11-year-old, Frank Epperson, invented the ice lolly (or popsicle if you're in the US). He had left a cup of powdered soda and water on his porch. After a very chilly night, Frank returned to find his 'pop' had frozen, with the stirrer stuck in the middle.

Instead of doing what most adults would have, which is moaning about the ruined soda and chucking it away, the 11-year-old's curious nature inspired him to grab the stirrer, pull the frozen mixture out of its cup and give it a lick to see if it still tasted good. And so, the popsicle was born.

So, use your sense of fun if you want to be more inventive. Play with ideas. Look at things differently and see if there are simpler ways of achieving things. Take some risks (but not as many risks as the 'Flying Tailor'). Explore new things, rather than dismissing them and look at mistakes to see how they might possibly be turned into a positive. And never let your childlike curiosity die.

Children Learn Less Consciously

Children are fabulous at learning. They absorb new information very quickly, and that is because they are often using their unconscious mind to do it.

Try to consciously ride a bike. I mean, really think about it. Which angle do your feet have to be at on the pedals? Where must your weight be spread in order to achieve balance? What amount of pressure must you exert on the pedals in order to move the wheels? If you tried to ride a bike by thinking deeply about it, I assure you, you'd fall off.

When adults learn something new, they go through a complex process of first consciously trying to do it, which can be a real struggle. It is only later that they move to an unconscious level of learning and are able to improve their performance effortlessly.

Think back to your very first driving lessons. In the beginning, you're following instructions about how to use the pedals, the steering wheel, the mirrors, and all the other equipment. You can pick out newbie drivers easily, because they will be the ones travelling at a snail's pace or weaving all over the road.

But after some time behind the wheel, you no longer have to think about how to do it. The information has been stored at an unconscious level. At that point, your driving should get better and better without you having to follow a manual or actively learn new skills (unless you're my sister, who has never quite grasped the phrase "Less speed, more haste").

When we learn less consciously, we can often pick up things at a faster rate than if we focused consciously on the task at hand.

Have you ever had an 'ear-worm', a song that goes round and round in your head and just won't stop? Thanks to PJ & Duncan's abysmal – and dreadfully catchy – tune *Let's get Ready to Rhumble*, I have. If you've never listened to it, I beg you, don't, or you may be tortured in a similar way to me.

Ear worms tend to be songs that we made no effort to learn, and we may not even like (no, I don't like it, PJ & Duncan), but have picked up because they were in our presence at an unconscious level.

Believe me, I made no conscious effort to learn that track and would even go and switch the radio to a different station if I ever noticed it playing. And yet I know every bit of that damn song, because it was at number nine in the charts when I was 14 and I was always listening to the radio.

There must have been numerous times when I was absorbed in something else and didn't even notice it playing in the background. So, the evil song sneakily leaked into my brain at an unconscious level and is now forever stuck there until the day I die. Thanks a bunch, brain. But you can use unconscious ways of learning to your advantage, just as children do.

Have you ever wondered why young children learn new languages more readily than adults? One of the reasons is because they don't sit there learning endless grammar rules. They simply match words to their meanings – and the grammar falls into place more or less unconsciously.

I'd never even heard of an adjective, adverb, clause, or the confounded 'dative case' until I was 17 and started my French and German A-levels. Yet, I had learned English perfectly well as a child without knowing any grammatical terms whatsoever.

It was a real struggle to learn German in particular, which has many different rules, tenses and cases. Our language assistant did something very clever to help us. She would bring German pop songs into class and encourage us to take them home to listen to. To this day, I can still remember the tunes and lyrics of all of Herbert Grönemeyer's greatest hits. As we covered new vocabulary in class, I started to realise what the lyrics meant too.

But it was only when I went to live in Berlin that I

became totally fluent, and sometimes even dreamed in German. That's because I was immersed in the language in so many unconscious ways. In shops and on the streets, I constantly heard people chattering away in German. The radio station playing in the local bar (where I was a live-in customer) broadcast in German. The billboards, street and store signs were in German. My brain couldn't help but absorb the lingo.

And I learned new words by matching them to their meaning, like children do when learning language. It was far more effective than translating them from the English, like we did at college.

For example, I'd go into the local bakery, where the pastries were all labelled in German, obviously. Now, I know a sausage roll when I see one. So it was simple for me to learn that *Würstchen im Schlafrock* meant "sausage roll" just by spotting it in the display. I was matching words to objects, just as kids do, without having to take the extra step of translating from the English in my mind.

In fact, if you *had* tried to translate the word "sausage roll" directly between German and English, you'd look like a total idiot. *Würstchen* literally means "little sausage", *im* means "in", and S*chlafrock* means "night attire". So, you would have ended up with "a little sausage in pyjamas" if you had looked up the words separately in a translation book. I guess it's the same as asking a German if they like "pigs in a blanket". They might be terribly disgusted or think you a little mad if you translated it literally.

In fact, I did make a huge mistake when I was first in Berlin and got very sick. I'll blame my weakened state for this error. I suffered from a bout of nausea, where I would gag all the time and sometimes even vomit. So, I went to the local doctor and tried to explain my symptoms – but not without first consulting my oh-so-handy translation book.

Instead of telling the doctor that I had been gagging, meaning retching, I told him I had been gagged. He must have been very confused and wondered why I was in a doctor's office instead of going to the police about the matter. It was only by resorting to charades, and eventually vomiting over his consultation couch, that the doctor understood my problem.

Another reason why little children learn languages more easily than adults is that they aren't afraid to make mistakes while they are practising. They are far less *self*-conscious than people who are older.

I remember cringing if I ever had to read something

out loud in my language classes as a teenager, and I would deliberately not produce the perfect accent, even though I knew how to, because I was afraid that the other students would think I was showing off or being pretentious.

But many little kids love to show off and will happily practise their language skills out loud. And doing this consolidates the information in their brain.

So, just by looking at languages, we can see how kids have an edge over adults. Next time you want to learn something, try using your unconscious mind to help you along.

If you want to learn a language, and don't really fancy emigrating, hypnosis tapes and playing foreign radio stations in the background could help you.

For other things you'd like to learn, don't over-focus or be frightened of making mistakes. And be less self-conscious. It doesn't matter what other people think.

Whenever I study anything, I always try to let my unconscious mind have plenty of opportunities to soak up information. You can do this by filling your environment with cues that your brain can't help but take in unconsciously.

Put information you want to learn in your peripheral vision. For example, stick relevant posters, pictures or post-it notes on your walls. Play a topical podcast or audiobook in the background while you attend to another task. Speed-reading and skimming passages, instead of trying to read every word consciously, can help you learn faster from text-based materials.

Adults know that any final decision or solution must be reasonable in order to work out. But if you start from that point, rather than finishing with it, you might just miss out on a ton of great ideas and a load of learning. So don't start out from an utterly fixed or 'sensible' point of view.

Learn from the wisdom of children. Be more flexible; allow yourself a few risks, 'mistakes' and adventures; look from fresh perspectives; have fun and play when you want to be creative; simplify things; let your unconscious mind assist you with learning.

Be childlike first, *then* let your adult mind modify and manage your ideas, adjusting for consequences and long-term effects. If you can do that, you will benefit enormously, and you will be much smarter as a result.

Boss Your Brain Around

We've already seen how easily the brain can be manipulated and how we can use this to our advantage – e.g. making it think we're exercising when really we're just lying on the sofa, eating chips.

There are many different ways to use tricks on the brain to instantly make it smarter. We can improve our memory, our ability to achieve goals, and boost our speed at completing tasks, all just by telling the brain what we want.

One of the major keys to unlocking superior cognitive performance is giving the brain some instructions and telling it where you want it to focus. That may sound simplistic, but some of the ways in which we can achieve this *are* ridiculously simple and easy to do. And several of these methods work in just seconds.

Say It Loud

My household loves cooking and our spice cupboard is bursting at the seams. But, naturally, some of us are less organised than others, so it often ends up in a jumble, with packets and jars stacked up randomly. Now, most spice packs look alike, so when you've got about 50 spices to sift through, it can take some time to locate which one you want – unless you use my super-special method of mumbling to yourself while looking for ingredients.

I know talking out loud to yourself is associated with madness, but if it is true that neurotics tend to talk to themselves more, it's just because they are trying to get more control over their brain. So, call me crazy if you like, but I can find the thyme more quickly than anyone else, because I tell my brain what to look for. If you're searching for an item, repeating what you're looking for out loud actually helps you to find it faster. And science has proven it.

In a 2012 study, researchers at Wisconsin-Madison University and Pennsylvania University turned a bunch of volunteers into 'super-searchers' simply by getting them to say the name of the item they were asked to look for out loud.

Participants could locate objects more quickly when they repeated what they were seeking to themselves. Speaking the name out loud increased participants' speed at finding household items, and also familiar brands and groceries when completing a virtual shop. So when I'm saying "thyme" to myself, I'm actually turning myself into an expert 'thyme-detector' for a short space of time.

So, how does this work? Attaching a verbal label to something makes that item less abstract and more concrete, helping your brain sharpen its focus. As a therapist, I have had clients shy away from talking about difficult problems, saying: "If I actually say it, that means it's really true". It seems these patients are intuitively avoiding this mechanism.

But, both in therapy, and in everyday life, we can use this process to our advantage. So, for example, if I want to help someone overcome the feelings of helplessness that trauma often causes, I could ask them to verbally tell me the ending first – i.e. how they escaped or survived – making their experience of courage and safety more vivid than the other, more difficult parts of the event.

Consider how you could use self-talk to give you a cognitive boost. It can help with many things, from finding your keys to speeding up learning.

If you're trying to learn a new task, talking yourself through it step by step guides your brain, allowing it to perform better. This is probably why, when my mum taught me how to tie my shoelaces, she made me repeat: "Under, over, inside, out." to myself. No, I had no friends at school because everyone thought I was weird. But, I did have excellently-laced shoes.

You can also use this 'abstract-to-concrete' tool to improve your memory or to remind someone else to do something. This works with others because even *hearing* an instruction aloud allows the brain to make concepts more real. This is why your old housemates always "forgot" what you wrote on your post-it notes about the milk. Shoulda just told them. A note only has writing. A verbal instruction has a voice, a tone, a cadence, a rhythm, perhaps an accent and much more to tie it to reality. Actors sometimes have tremendous difficulty remembering lines when reading them on a page, but rehearsing out loud makes it much easier.

But, back to telling people what to do. Follow the rule of three here: say whatever needs to be remembered to yourself, or someone else, three times, to make it stick. If you're worried you'll come across as nagging when doing this with someone else, you don't have to say it the same way each time, as long as the core message remains the same.

This works even better if you can tie an action to the item to be remembered. It sets up a chain reaction in the brain, where doing one thing will remind you, or the other person, to do something else. Here's an example: "As you open the front door, pick up your keys from the table." Again, repeat it three times, varying your language slightly if necessary.

This is even better than just saying: "Keys; remember the keys; pick up the door keys". Why? Because you don't want to suddenly remember the keys when you are already out, or you'll be smacking your forehead in the supermarket only then realising that you forgot them, at the same time as repeating: "apples, apples, apples" to yourself, and looking like a right fruitloop.

Use a cue to remember your keys which occurs *before* you leave home, like opening the front door. You should get a message from your brain to collect the keys as soon as you touch the door handle.

You Just Gotta Believe

If you're familiar with the Law of Attraction, you may have heard some ludicrous things about it, like that constantly focussing on a Ferrari, and just believing you will get one, will eventually attract a brand new Lusso straight to your driveway. I have some very sad news for you. Ain't gonna happen.

But just because some people have discredited the LoA with some ridiculous claims and horribly cheesy films, it doesn't mean that there isn't any truth to the idea that we can attain what we want by using the power of our minds.

Positive beliefs, focus, and setting goals for our brains to work towards, *can* help us get what we want. For example, I'm going to tell you right now that it *is* possible to become smarter and more intelligent if you want to. Your mental capabilities aren't fixed. You can push your brain to achieve its utmost potential with many of the methods taught in this very book and others in the Wiseism series.

Why have I told you that (apart from plugging my other books)? Because science has shown it to be true. And research has also revealed that if you believe that you are able to become smarter, you will.

Psychologists at Stanford University split a bunch of schoolkids into two groups. One group was told that learning changes the brain and were given positive statements indicating that the students had the ability to improve their own intelligence. The second group were told that intelligence could not be changed, and no matter how hard they worked at a subject, if they just weren't good at it, they would never improve.

Both groups took a test based on a seminar they had

attended. The students who had been told that they could change their own intelligence scored 85 per cent on the test, compared to just 54 per cent for those who were taught that they couldn't influence their own innate intelligence levels. So, the power of belief really does matter when it comes to achieving better cognitive performance.

While some of the LoA crowd may give a different explanation for it, the truth is that being more confident and motivated will have greatly influenced how the students performed. If you don't believe you can become smarter, why would you even try to?

But it is not just positive beliefs about intelligence that can help you perform better at all sorts of things. All beliefs influence the way we think, act, and our ability to get the results we want.

Your brain takes cues from what you believe and will alter its neural pathways to reflect that. So, if you believe you are no good at public speaking, for example, and keep telling yourself that, then you are probably going to choke when you have to do a speech or presentation.

Conversely, if you believe you can create a better, wiser life, your brain will co-operate with that belief, making it easier for neural connections to form that will help you with that goal. Your brain will also be on the look-out for more opportunities, and ways to help you succeed.

Just as with verbal labelling, your beliefs can be made more concrete by repeatedly speaking them aloud. And that's not out of a Rocky film. Research carried out by Exeter University showed that people who consistently tell themselves they can achieve a goal are more likely to succeed.

Intention!

Whenever you give your brain messages about what you want, you're directing it to focus in a certain way. It will then actively look for information and answers to assist you in attaining your goals.

Here is an example of this very mechanism in action, which we've probably all experienced at some point when chatting with our friends. Have you ever been talking about movie, but can't remember who played a certain character? You can picture the actor's face, can't you? And you can even list other films they've starred in. But your memory draws a blank when it comes to recalling their name. So, you appeal to your friends with: "Oh, you know, thingamajig, what's-his-name, the one with the beard. Had more divorces than Liz Taylor. Always looks like he's swallowed a wasp."

After giving your puzzled friends increasingly cryptic clues, you're still none the wiser. In exasperation, you shout to yourself: "Oh, what was his name?!" Finally, you give up. It was a stupid movie anyway. Then, long after you've forgotten all about the conversation, the actor's name magically pops into your mind. And you also realise, "Oh wait, he doesn't have a beard actually". No wonder your friends didn't have a clue who you were talking about.

Well, where did that come from? Why did you recall his name now, of all times, when you're just about to go to bed?

When you asked the question "What was his name?", your brain listened. It took your request and helpfully continued searching your memory banks to retrieve the knowledge you required. And when it found the information, your brain shared it with you in a calm moment. Your brain also took the trouble to remind you, that, no, he didn't have a beard. And it did all that because you made it clear that you wanted your question answered. Good brain. Have a cookie.

If you're ever wondering how to figure something out, ask your brain the question before you go to bed. Often you'll wake up with an immediate solution, or the answer will come to you later on in the day.

Your brain can be really helpful as long as you tell it precisely what you want. In addition to giving your brain a direct message by verbally labelling what you want to know or achieve, you can help the brain out by giving it material it especially likes to work with – vivid mental imagery.

This is another technique that LoA proponents favour. They like to form vivid mental pictures of what they want to 'manifest' in their lives. Some of them create picture boards plastered with images of things they desire or carry a symbol with them that represents what they want. No matter what anyone says, carrying a self-written cheque for $10million in his wallet did not 'manifest' Jim Carrey his fortune. It may well have motivated him, but his mindset, hard work and skills were what made him mega-bucks.

Although these techniques do tell the brain what you would like it to focus on, doing this alone will not magically bring you your heart's desires. While your brain can give you what's already stored in your memory, if you want something that's not already there, it will take a bit more effort. You can not say to your brain: "Speak French!" while picturing the Eiffel Tower and carrying a baguette in your bag in the hope that you will learn the language out of thin air.

So, when you do tell your brain what you want, be aware that you are only setting an intention, allowing it to be guided in a certain direction. However, the areas of the brain involved in intention are closely connected to those linked with action. So, by setting an intention, you are actually more likely to act on it.

Using visualisation is a good way of setting clear and compelling intentions and getting your brain to back up your plans. Remember that the brain does not always know the difference between the imagination and reality.

A 2009 study by the Institute of Neurology, London, revealed that imagined experiences used many of the same brain regions that activate when recalling a real autobiographical memory. When either a real past event or a fictitious scene was vividly evoked by the volunteers in the study, many networks of the brain were involved, including those needed for navigation, and sense of space and place.

The more richly you use your imagination, adding in

lots of details, including sounds, smells and other sensory information, the more likely your brain is to view it as an actual experience.

There is much evidence that visualising certain things regularly, particularly while in a hypnotic state, can influence things to with your own body. We saw this with exercise, and people have been able to increase everything from muscle tone to breast size purely by using vivid mental imagery.

There is also evidence that people have been able to overcome illnesses by visualising their antibodies as strong and dominant and by imagining diseased cells being attacked or shrinking, for example. The body and mind are intrinsically connected, so it is possible to directly affect your body just by using your mind.

However, there are more steps involved if you want to get what you desire in the external world, because you are not a magical magnet that can pull exactly what you want towards you.

So think of vivid visualisation as a tool to motivate you, to guide the brain to seek out opportunities, and to help you consider the actions and decisions you need to take to achieve your desires.

Mental Rehearsal

Detailed mental landscapes can be explored, just like the real world, giving you the opportunity to 'pre-experience' the future. Enacting potential scenarios in your mind allows you to assess their viability. You can modify the images to see if other ways of doing things might be better.

Sports stars use this tool all the time in order to train the brain to perform and to improve strategy. You can use it, too, to create wise plans and schemes that will draw you nearer to your desired outcomes.

Visualising gives your brain a substantial work-out, as well, since it involves many cognitive processes. Doing it will keep your brain sharp and creative. The Institute of Neurology study authors wrote that this ability to construct an imaginary scenario, then evaluate it, "sits near the apex of human intellectual abilities", letting us be limitlessly inventive.

I use this method in one of the other Wiseism books, *How to Create Your Ideal Life*, because it's so powerful. Combining motivation, brain-guiding, creativity and practical strategies, mental rehearsal is the ideal tool to concoct an ingenious plan for success.

Copycatting

There is a cool short-cut we can exploit when we want to learn something more quickly, or attract people to us that will help us achieve our goals.

Have you heard of 'mirror neurons'? They are called that because they cause us to unconsciously mirror the behaviour or feelings of people we are observing. What mirror neurons actually do is start to activate the same areas of our brain that have activated in the person you are watching.

Have you ever hung around someone with a really strong accent and found that, after a while, you end up talking like them? While it's totally embarrassing, especially if the other person notices, this is the power of mirror neurons at work.

But you can use your mirror neurons in productive and positive ways if you know what you're doing. For example, if you want to learn a particular physical skill more quickly, don't just read about it in a book. Watch someone doing it instead. Your mirror neurons will cause your brain's pre-motor and parietal cortex to activate. These regions boost attention and prepare the body to move, making you ready to perform the skill, too. This process can actually cause a simulation of the skill to occur in our brain, making it easier for us to actually perform the task, even if it is new.

Emotions are also affected by mirror neurons, which explains why stress and laughter can be contagious. And now you understand why, even if you aren't scared of spiders, when the person next to you starts totally freaking out at the sight of one, you also start to feel panicky. Until you see that they are screaming about a tiddly little arachnid and either laugh at them or kindly move the spider outside. Do the second one – you'll earn karma points.

You can use your mirror neurons to 'steal' skills from other people and guide your brain to smarter states. Hang around folks whose states you'd like to pick up on, and their attributes will start to rub off on you. Nick a bit of your mate's charisma or your colleague's confidence. Naturally, you'll want to make sure there is someone really wise in your crew.

Now you know what mirror neurons can do, you will probably want to avoid negative and stressy people, so that their states don't colour your mood or quash your cognitive abilities.

We can also use our own states to activate mirror neurons in others. How can this help us to become smarter? Well, two brains are usually better than one. And if you want others to help or teach you, first convey an attitude of helpfulness yourself.

Be a positive, kind and generous person, and people around you will be more likely to act in the same way. If you make others feel happy, they will be keener to help you out. They will respond more positively to being asked for favours which can move you forward on your quest for wisdom and success.

So be especially positive, open and giving to people you want to learn from, which will encourage them to share their knowledge with you. I'm not promoting manipulation of other people here. Helping makes the world go round and it should be a reciprocal process that benefits everyone. The more good stuff we share, the better we all become.

To summarise, don't be afraid of being a bit bossy to your brain. When you tell it want you want or need, either directly or indirectly, it likes to be helpful. Just as a pupil will not fulfil their potential if they are never guided or directed, your brain benefits from you teaching it how to maximise its capacity and use its innate abilities better.

Glad All Over

Gather around, everybody. I'd like to tell you a story about the happiest day of my life. No, it wasn't Man United's victory over Bayern. As much as it made me happy, my experience was slightly marred by me jumping up and down on a chair with joy – and breaking it.

The happiest day of my life was when I walked out of a therapist's office. I was so euphoric, I literally skipped down the street – yes, real people do this if they are truly joyful and don't mind what others think. I didn't mind, because I had just been cured of a crippling anxiety disorder that had haunted me for years.

My disorder had truly ruined my life. I was unable to do normal things like shopping or eating out without sweating and shaking with fear. I was scared of doing anything that might draw attention to me. It had got so bad that I couldn't even leave the house without having an alcoholic drink or seven to calm me down.

I had suffered from this illness for roughly a decade. I'd seen loads of shrinks, counsellors and psychs with no positive results whatsoever. But my new therapist cured me in just 90 minutes. Trembling, I had walked into his office with my head down, perspiring enough to fill a paddling pool. I walked out with a broad grin across my face, head held high and the happiest I had ever been in my entire life.

It was truly wonderful to be able to stride (and skip) down the street looking at the amazing world around me, rather than shuffling along quickly with my eyes fixed on the pavement and my heart beating like a drum on steroids.

The second best day of my life was waking up the next morning and realising that it had not just been a dream or a temporary fix, but that I was now totally free from the horrible dread that had plagued me for so many years.

I tested out everything that I hadn't been able to do before. It was utterly awesome to discover that all the things I used to panic about were now effortless. I felt so confident, I was on top of the world.

Now, that's a lovely story, isn't it? And I hope your mirror neurons were making you smile about it too.

By writing out that happy story and sharing it with you, my lovely reader, we have both become a bit smarter. Bonus! But, I'm sure you'll now be curious as to why that is the case.

When you feel good, you instantly become better at a range of tasks. Being happy allows you to think faster and more intelligently, as well as boosting your ability to learn. That's good news, because who doesn't like being happy? Apart from Oscar the Grouch.

So, think of a happy story from your own life before reading on, to ensure you can absorb the information in this chapter.

Back? OK, let's begin...

Anything that makes us feel upbeat and positive can cause us to be cleverer. But, why? It's mainly down to that brain chemical dopamine again. When we feel buzzed, dopamine is released into all the right places in our brain that help us think, work and learn more effectively.

You may think you already know what presses your happy buttons, but as we'll discover later, people are often mistaken when asked to predict what will make them happiest. So read this chapter thoroughly and try out all the suggestions to make sure you are not missing out on some really positive stuff.

And if you're down in a bad way, like I was with my anxiety disorder, there are some neat tricks you can use to lift your spirits, even if everything seems bleak. So, let's get into those quick mood-boosters now, just in case any of you need to lift a Charlie Brown-style cloud of gloom right-away.

Fun Fixes

Simply Smile

We're bossing the brain around again and using its inability to separate fact from fiction. Whenever you smile, your brain thinks you must be happy. And it responds by flooding you with feel-good chemicals. Nice brain. Have another cookie.

If you're really down in the dumps and can't even manage a grin, try a half-smile. It will give you less of a mood boost, but you will still see some benefits.

Trick Your Eyes

How can wearing sun-glasses make you happy? Well, squinting uses some of the same muscles as frowning. If you screw up your eyes against the light, you may feel sad, or even angry. Because your brain thinks you are, it will dump out corresponding stress chemicals. Silly brain. Give me back that cookie.

Popping on a pair of shades lets you open your eyes wider, preventing your brain from sabotaging a nice, sunny day by thinking you must be stressed. Ah, here come the feel-good chemicals again.

Get Plant Power

We already know that nature has relaxing properties. People in rural areas rate their happiness levels more highly than those living in the city. But if you can't get to the park or there isn't a nature trail nearby, you can cheat by bringing the outdoors inside.

Research led by Cardiff University shows that placing plants in offices causes a 30 per cent rise in workplace satisfaction. Workers with a pot plant complete tasks faster without compromising on accuracy. So, pop a nice plant in any rooms where you spend lots of time.

Try Colour Therapy

Vibrant colours make us more capable and positive, according to research from the University of Essex.

When exposed to sunny shades, volunteers scored up

to 25 per cent higher in mental agility tests than those who were shown the colour grey. Brighter tones also improved hand-eye co-ordination by 20 per cent. Intense reds can ease depression and raise confidence, while bright blue lowers stress. I'm now considering painting my walls blue, as another study showed that people make fewer typos when in a blue room.

Gladiator, Ready...

Physical fights release dopamine in the brain, giving us a buzz and helping us learn. A study at Vanderbilt University revealed that mice actively sought out fights after just one instance of having to see off an intruder mouse in their home cage. These mice had learned to love having a brawl.

I don't advise going around battering others, unless a giant mouse starts on you of course. You can get your dopamine hit without fear of arrest by pounding a punchbag or doing contact sports like martial arts.

Watch Comedies – Or Tragedies

Here's a strange one. Clearly, watching a funny film is likely to make you feel good. But a study by Ohio State University showed that seeing tearjerkers makes many of us happier too. Researchers forced hundreds of students to sit through the eye-wateringly bleak movie *Atonement* and gauged their responses before, during, and after the film. They found that many of the students felt happier after they had watched it. Not because they were sadists, but because it made them reflect on their close positive relationships.

One caveat: the students who didn't feel happier after seeing the film tended to have ego-centric thoughts, such as: "At least *my* life isn't as bad as that", rather than thinking of people in their lives who made them happy and counting their blessings.

Be Upbeat

A myth has prevailed for many years, suggesting that listening to Mozart makes you smarter. The legend started after research by the University of California at Irvine revealed that some students were better at spatial-reasoning after hearing a Mozart Sonata than after being given relaxation instructions or sitting still before testing.

But there is no magic to Mozart. Students could do just as well on spatial-reasoning tests by listening to a passage from a Steven King novel, which is exactly what some other researchers proved. The key to doing better lay in whether or not volunteers enjoyed what they had heard. The mood boost made students score better, not Mozart.

Other studies show that energetic music helps kids to perform better on certain tasks – again, because it lifted their spirits. So, if you're not in the Mozart fan club, don't despair. Throw on some music you enjoy to give your brain a boost. Note that these effects only last for about 15 minutes after the music stops; what a great excuse to play your favourite track again.

Snuggle Up

Your partner is sure to like this one. Cuddling makes us happier, because it releases the hormone oxytocin, which makes us feel warm and blissed-out. Taking it several steps further, making love is one of the most fun and healthy ways of boosting dopamine.

Sex also helps the hippocampus create new neurons, making your long-term memory better. In one study, women were asked to analyse abstract words. Ladies who engaged in regular lovin' remembered the words better than those going through a 'dry spell'.

Reasons To Be Cheerful

Now that we have covered the quick tricks to increase

your positive emotions, let us move onto what you should regularly include in your life to make you feel happier and be smarter every day.

While you can use short-term tricks to lift your mood, prioritising your happiness should be daily habit if you're aiming for peak performance. You really can't lose when you make your mental wellbeing of utmost importance. You'll enjoy life so much more, will be an absolute pleasure to hang out with, and you'll become smarter, wiser and more successful, too.

It is not success that leads to happiness. You can still be miserable and depressed even if, from the outside, you seem to have it all. It is happiness that leads to success, which is what very few people realise. When you are happier, you are smarter and perform better – it's as simple as that.

At the beginning of this chapter, I used one method of making you feel happier by getting you to remember a wonderful past experience. When we recall, or write out, events that have made us smile, we relive them to a certain extent, making us even happier.

Happiness is a precious resource, so don't waste it by only experiencing lovely things once. Double your joy by journaling or remembering wonderful things that have happened. This technique is especially powerful if you recall recent moments of happiness, perhaps the best thing that happened to you today, or the most meaningful or fun experience you have had in the past 24 hours.

There are a few reasons why this tool works best with recent events. Firstly, they will be fresh in your mind, enabling you to recall the rich details, making them feel more real. Secondly, if you're in the midst of a low period, it can help to pick out the positives, no matter how small or large they may be. And if you've really got the blues, thinking of a time in the distant past when you were happier may lead you to compare that with where you are now, making you even more upset about the state of your life.

Make it a daily habit to write down three things you are grateful for and your happiest moment of the day. Doing this will give you a brain boost and also help you to build positivity into a daily practice. If you do this, you'll find it easier to detect and cherish the smaller pieces of everyday happiness as well as times when you experience overwhelming joy.

So far, my best moment today was actually having a laugh with my postman. Probably because I've been alone all day, writing.

Do you think that's a bit weak? I don't. I can really appreciate that small interaction and smile back on it gratefully, because I have firmly trained my positivity muscles and can hone in on even the tiniest bits of pleasure and appreciate them fully.

And the three things I am the most grateful for today: Coffee, the sun shining through the window, and the leftover curry sitting on the table ready for me to eat. Hey, it's not even noon and I have already got all these wonderful things to make me smile.

So even if you are lonely, down in the dumps, or have experienced negative things in your life, it doesn't mean you can't train your brain to note the positives. Some people believe that this is impossible, and that you're either a pessimist or an optimist, and that's just the way it is (those people are generally pessimists). But nothing could be further from the truth.

I am living proof that you can change your outlook just by training your brain, no matter what you used to think and whatever struggles you've gone through, or are still facing, in your life.

I know this to be true because I was an incredibly negative person in the past. I wish I had known that it was possible to change how I viewed things when I had anxiety and alcohol problems, because that was a truly miserable part of my life.

And while I did have many genuinely horrific events and experiences back then, if I'd trained my positivity muscles a little sooner, I would have been able to pick out some things to be happy about too. That would have made me not only a happier person, but also a more motivated and capable one. I might have seen a wise way out of my troubles and ended them faster.

But I did finally start working on my attitude, and I can tell you what a big difference it makes, especially when the chips are down.

I'm afraid I'm going to have to tell you something a bit sad in order to prove my point. But don't worry, there is a happy ending to it, as you will see.

So, after years of being too scared to go outside, and then several more years where my struggle to beat alcoholism meant I often suffered severe withdrawals that left me bed-bound in agony, shaking, sweating, hallucinating and vomiting for up to a week, when I was finally free of all those things it felt like heaven.

After my recovery, I was one of the happiest people

around. I was so grateful that I was now free to live my life and every day I felt blessed. During this time, I achieved many things of which I am very proud. My life was truly wonderful and I enjoyed it to the full.

Spin on a few years. I am now writing this book while stuck in bed with a very debilitating illness, which I have now had for the past three years.

My malady causes me physical pain and affects my mobility, vision, concentration and various other vital faculties, so much so that I can not currently see any therapy clients, nor even go across town to visit my friends. Even writing this book is a struggle as I have to stop for days, or even weeks, at a time if my illness gets the better of me. I used to be a writing machine and could happily knock out several chapters in one sitting without flagging at all.

When I got ill, it was almost like having my anxiety disorder back. My life now is severely limited again in many of the same ways as before, not due to fear this time, but because of my physical symptoms.

It would have been easy for me to get very depressed, having gone from a terrible affliction, to being cured and free, only to return to a state of confinement once more. It seems an unfair thing to happen to someone who has already endured and overcome so much.

And during this time, my beloved cat, nearly 15 years my companion through thick and thin, died. I was heart-broken because I loved her so much and now she isn't around to cuddle on days when I am alone and incapacitated. I have had terrible sciatica from being bed-bound, which left me sleepless and in pain for days. A medication I tried badly compromised my immunity, which led to me contracting pneumonia and developing sepsis, which sent me into intensive care and very nearly killed me.

I won't list all the other unpleasant things that have happened during my illness, because it isn't a positive thing to do, but suffice to say it has been a rough ride. And yet I am still happy and motivated. Why?

For the past three years, I have focused on the things I *am* still capable of, and counted my blessings and the things I am grateful for, rather than being miserable about my lot in life. While I have natural moments of sadness about the things I have lost and the stuff I am, once again, unable to do, I have trained my brain to be happier and more grateful. So, instead of sitting here sobbing, as the old me would have, I am writing this book instead.

I have what many people would term 'good' days and 'bad' days, which I just call fluctuations in symptoms. This means that sometimes I can see well, but can not concentrate, and other days I may be bed-bound, but my mental powers can be sharp as long as I sit very still and the room is darkened. So, if my mobility is weak, but my concentration isn't bad, I can write from my bed. How wonderful that I can still help people through my writing and books, even though I can't see clients face-to-face.

And when my ability to make sense of sentences goes completely out of the window, I can learn instead – learning is one of my great passions, and that hasn't been taken from me. Even when I am too cross-eyed to read, I can listen to educational podcasts, audio-books and videos.

I have never been as grateful for delivery services as I am now. I can get almost anything I need driven right to my door. And despite having gone through some poor doctors, I am grateful to have found a really understanding doctor and great specialist support.

Some of the people close to me have come into their own and will help me out when I can't do something as simple as cooking a meal or posting a letter, and I am endlessly thankful for them.

When my cat died, and I was deeply upset, a man I had previously helped with an addiction drove me to his tattooist and paid for me to have a tribute tattoo of her. That kindness and the sense that I still have my beautiful cat close to me immediately ended my grief. I truly have some superstars in my life.

So, even though I have lost a lot, I still have the ability to do some of the things I love. I also have a roof over my head, my bed, a computer, an internet connection and some amazing people I can count on. But most of all, I have my attitude, which is why I can still be happy in spite of all the pain, and despite the fact that this is not what I would have chosen to be my life.

Research has shown that 'happy' people report more positive events in their lives than 'unhappy' people. "Well, duh," you might think, weeping to think that taxpayers' money may have funded those studies.

However, what the research tellingly revealed is that those who were happy did *not* report fewer negative experiences than their unhappy counterparts. Just as many sad and bad things had befallen them as befell unhappy people, but the happy people were able to note the good things in their lives as well, while those who were generally unhappy didn't.

A review of numerous studies shows that a person's circumstances only account for a tiny fraction of their overall happiness levels (no more than 15 per cent). What counts much more than status, wealth or health is the way people view themselves and their lives.

Those who can find humour in adversity, reappraise negative situations, and focus on getting goals – not avoiding failure – are happier people, a 2001 review by the University of California found. Using these positive strategies made them smarter too.

Those who ruminated on poor past performance, or were overly critical of themselves, were unhappy and more likely to fail at their next task than those who were positive. Dwelling on negatives causes a brain drain. People who do it take longer to complete tests, read more slowly and have poorer comprehension levels than those who don't review their performance pessimistically.

So, start looking for the positives in yourself and your life, find ways to adapt to 'disasters' to make them manageable, and thank anyone who does you a good deed, big or small, and you'll not only be happier, but smarter as well.

And since happiness breeds success, it becomes like a benign cycle, enhancing your confidence, motivation levels and mood. This will help you to succeed again and again, and achieve bigger and better things.

And...Sleep

No, I'm not about to hypnotise you, although we will touch on that topic later. I'm just making sure that you're getting adequate rest.

It's common knowledge that sleep is crucial for many reasons, including performing well and being smart. In this chapter, we will delve deeper into the facts, bust some myths, and discover when, where and how to sleep to get the most out of your mind.

Having a decent kip does make you instantly smarter, as the effects can be felt as soon as you wake up. You will be aware of this, especially if you've ever tried to go to school or work after staying up all night. I know this horrific experience from my past when I used to suffer from poor sleep due to my drinking.

You drag yourself in with your eyes goggling, head aching and perhaps even a little drool coming out of your mouth. Focus, logic, concentration? What *are* those things? Are they even words? You end up doing little except counting the hours until you can escape. And when you finally get home, you throw yourself on the bed, kiss the pillow with pure relief, and swear never to forgo your precious sleep again.

In the morning, you congratulate yourself for sleeping for a few extra hours to catch up. But even though the drooling has stopped and you're no longer begging for the day to be over, you may feel a little fuzzy and will be off your game.

Sorry to spoil the party, but if you have a bad night's sleep, sleeping for longer the next day *doesn't* restore you to your best. 'Catch-up sleep' does not work as well as people believe. Your performance continues to suffer until you've slept properly for a few days. Even if you don't notice it, scientists have. According to a study, it takes a while to recover from a lack of sleep, especially if you don't sleep well on consecutive days.

The very worst sleep pattern of all is one that a lot of people have nowadays. Namely, waking themselves up with an alarm on workdays and sleeping in at the weekend to recover. If you have to force yourself to wake during the week, then you haven't slept enough and should go to bed earlier. This will improve your mental sharpness during the day.

So, if it's late, put this book down and get some shut-eye. Then you can contrast that horrible feeling sleep deprivation gives you with the refreshing boost that a decent rest brings. Can you remember waking up in the morning feeling so good that you practically leapt out of bed? That is the gift that quality sleep gives you. You feel positive, energetic, and your mind is much clearer.

It can be tempting to pull an all-nighter when you've got an important task to complete, but you're better off going to bed and finishing in the morning when your energy is restored and your mind is sharper.

This is also true when you're trying to study or revise. Sleep consolidates memory, so you should always rest after learning something new if you want it to stick – or at least take a break before studying any more.

Having a good kip also helps us to solve problems. In 2004, researchers at the University of Lübeck proved it. They devised a number game that could be learned with practice, but it had a hidden rule which made it easier to learn. It was akin to the multiplication tables. You can memorise them parrot-fashion, but when you know the patterns, you'll be much quicker at maths.

The researchers split volunteers into two groups after they had played the game for a while. One group was allowed an eight-hour sleep, while the other wasn't. When re-starting the game, volunteers who had slept uncovered the hidden rule twice as fast as those who had remained awake.

So, is eight hours the optimum amount of sleep for being on the ball? That's a commonly-held belief, but it's actually a myth. An individual's need for sleep will depend on their genetics, age, gender, health and many other variables – including some that might surprise you.

Under-sleepers

The quantity of sleep isn't everything. Some of the top performers in the world do very well on far less than eight hours. The quality and timing of your sleep may be more important factors for your functioning. Even your beliefs could play a part in how many hours of kip you need.

For example, Bill Clinton only slept about five hours a night when he was US president because he was told by one of his college professors that great men never need more than five hours of sleep.

We could question the former president's judgment on certain matters. But, Clinton is a shrewd man with an exceptional memory, even if he did 'forget' about incidents (that you'd think he'd remember) involving "that woman". Allegedly.

And Willie Geist really knows how to boss his brain about. When the MSNBC news anchor had to get up at 3:30am to present his early morning show, he kept himself alert by tricking his mind. Geist stated in Bloomsberg Businessweek that he often got only four hours of sleep. If he found himself flagging, he'd simply tell himself that he had got a full night of shut-eye. He claimed this made him immediately feel great and able to perform at his best.

You can not question the intelligence of inventors like Benjamin Franklin, Thomas Edison and Nikola Tesla – and yet these geniuses got by on only five, four and a mere two hours of sleep a night, respectively.

Most 'under-sleepers' seem to know a few tricks that may make high performance possible, so let's have a look at those.

After reviewing the habits of smart, successful people who don't sleep much, it is evident that lots of them share similar morning routines.

Exercise is a very common feature – as we know, this boosts oxygen levels in the brain. Meditation is also a popular choice and is a good way to prepare for the busy day ahead. It calms the body, gets rid of excess cortisol, improves focus and promotes deep thought.

Most under-sleepers never miss breakfast, and they don't just grab a bowl of Cheerios as they rush out of the door. A balanced breakfast with good fats, lots of protein and some healthy carbohydrates is the typical way for under-sleepers to start the day.

A common method under-sleepers use to revitalise themselves is the nap. You're better off grabbing 10 or 15 winks at a time, rather than fabled 40, since you risk creeping into the deep sleep zone if you nap for any longer. Waking up when you're fast asleep, rather than just dozing, can make you groggy and lethargic.

The UK Sleep Research Council recommends having a cup of coffee before a nap. As caffeine takes about 20 minutes to kick in, the coffee should wake you from your nap and help you feel even more alert at just the right time.

Timing could also be an important factor in under-sleepers' success. Most high-achievers in the modern world go to bed no later than 11pm. It is believed that the most restorative sleep occurs from 10pm to 2am.

While this is not necessarily true, there may be some

wisdom in "early to bed, early to rise". Our body works on Circadian rhythms, which can be affected by levels of light. Before Edison mucked up our sleep schedules by inventing the lightbulb, people used to sleep when the day darkened and wake up when the sun rose. It seems natural to conclude that the body was programmed to sleep in that way.

Super-sleepers

The largest amount of sleep demanded by someone clever and famous is probably the 11 hours former US president Calvin Coolidge needed per night. He was such a quiet man in office that you may not have noticed when he was awake or asleep, so that may be a myth. But he had a very sharp mind, having been a lawyer, and he excelled at debating. So, maybe he did need all that sleep after all.

Einstein firmly believed in the brain-boosting powers of slumber. He indulged in a 10-hour snooze-athon each night and regular naps during the day.

Some people wrongly assume that you can oversleep, perhaps after having experienced fatigue on waking up after a long sleep. In reality, that doesn't happen as long as you don't wake up in the middle of a sleep cycle, the first of which lasts 90 minutes on average.

Over the course of the night, cycles become longer, increasing to 120 minutes. During the cycle, you drift from light sleep into deep sleep and then the final Rapid Eye Movement, or REM, stage, known as the 'dream state'. This cycle repeats itself over and over again and, as long as you're not awoken from deep sleep, you won't feel foggy if you sleep for longer.

Sleeping more could improve your fluid intelligence – the ability to correlate new information with things you already know, helping you to solve problems, rationalise, and identify patterns.

When our bodies are in non-REM sleep, the brain has 'spindle events': short, sharp bursts of brain-wave activity. Research shows that the more spindle events you have, the better your fluid IQ. While we don't know whether this is a mere correlation or if spindles actually give people better logic skills, there are other benefits to having more sleep, too.

Dream On

Prolonged sleep increases REM-sleep states, meaning you will dream more often. As the length of the sleep cycle rises, so does the length of dream states, while non-REM sleep becomes shorter. This partly happens as the non-REM states are when our bodily functions are restored and refreshed. So, once your body has finished its physical upkeep tasks, it leaves you free to dream more often.

People often wonder why we dream, and no-one knows the answer for sure. But dreaming *must* be fundamental to our lives, since studies have shown that everyone does it, whether they can remember their dreams or not. It is also notable that when individuals suffer from severe sleep deprivation, their bodies will force them into the REM-state. When this happens, people start to dream whilst awake, causing hallucinations.

The most infamous case of this may be that of DJ Peter Tripp, who stayed awake for 200 hours for a publicity stunt...ahem...charity appeal. Scientists kept the radio presenter under observation to ensure he wasn't in danger and didn't doze off. At the 120-hour mark, Tripp literally started tripping, seeing flames shooting out of a chest of drawers and believing that one of the researchers, who was dourly dressed, was an undertaker who'd come to bury him.

He then thought these were tricks by the scientists who were trying to frame him for a crime. Tripp *had* actually committed a crime, for which he had not yet been caught – taking bribes to play certain songs on his show – so his waking dreams may have been an indicator of his underlying anxiety about that.

Dreams clearly have an important role in our lives – and even the most nonsensical of dreams have a function, whether it is your brain performing mental housekeeping or trying to give you messages to help you solve problems.

Because dreams occur in the unconscious mind, they can be a wonderful source of wisdom, a spur for creativity, and there are many instances of dreams inspiring novel things and helping to find solutions when the conscious mind is stuck.

Einstein claimed that the theory of special relativity occurred after analysing a dream about cows being electrocuted. No, I'm not sure what frying bovine has to do with physics, either. But he credited this dream with kicking off an entirely fresh chain of thought, which led to many mental breakthroughs. No wonder Einstein was the king of sleeping.

Elias Howe managed to break through a brain block when he was trying to invent the sewing machine. He couldn't work out where to place the eye in the needle to make it work properly. During his frustration, he dreamed he was captured and repeatedly stabbed by cannibals – he noticed that their spears had a hole at the tip, and Howe's design problem was solved.

Dmitri Mendeleev was struggling to work out how chemical elements fit together, and had some inkling that their arrangement might have something to do with atomic weight. But it wasn't until he fell asleep that he was able to create the Periodic Table.

"I saw in a dream a table where all the elements fell into place as required," the chemist explained. He was then able to use the table to predict the properties of some elements, which had not even been formally discovered at the time.

The REM state is responsible for artistic creations as well. Paul McCartney found the tune to *Yesterday* in his dreams. Director James Cameron literally dreamt up the movie *Terminator*. Author Stephen King claims many of his ideas for novels have been inspired by his dreams, including *Misery* and *Dreamcatcher*, ironically. That man must have some horrible nightmares.

Dreams are great for analysing your performance too. Golfer Jack Nicklaus was struggling with his game until he dreamed that he played a perfect round. In the dream, the Masters Champion had been gripping the club in a different way. He tried out the grip in real life and, bingo, he instantly improved.

Not every dream will lead to great insights. Often we dream about rather mundane things that happened in our day. But always look out for clues, especially if the dream recurs or sticks in your mind.

Don't go and buy a bunch of 'Dream Interpretation' books. Most of them full of garbage, like if you dream that your teeth are falling out, then it means you're about to lose some money. In my humble opinion, such a dream is much more likely to reflect a concern about health or ageing. Don't you think? I mean, what have teeth got to with cash? Anyone?

I tend to be pretty good at interpreting dreams, so I'll give you some tips on how to do it. Analysing your dreams well involves distinguishing what is relevant, contextual, and irrelevant.

When I was doing my A-levels at college, a friend of mine dreamt that we were at the pub and there were three pint glasses on the table. Two were full of beer and one was almost empty. It sounds like quite a dull dream, doesn't it? Unless you have a fetish for glass or truly love beer. But the dream was very vivid and it bothered my friend and she couldn't work out why.

So, I put the dream into context. We spent lots of time in the pub when at college. We had a local bar just up the road from the building and would often visit at lunch. So that was a natural setting for the dream to occur in, and linked it to college. My friend was doing three A-levels at the time, and she had spoken briefly of feeling confident about doing well in two of them, but feeling she might fail the third.

When put into context, it's obvious what her dream meant. It was a reflection of her concern about the third subject she was studying. Moreover, her brain was telling her that she needed to put more effort into the course she was struggling with, while focusing less on the two she had already mastered.

So, the beer itself was irrelevant, in that it her dream had nothing to do with alcohol. Instead, it was a way of representing her studies. The pub was linked with college, giving me a clue to where to start looking for relevance. Then, mulling over what was going on in her life, led me easily to the conclusion.

If you have a dream that you can't seem to shake, think about the challenges in your life and see how the dream may fit in. Even more importantly, look for wisdom the dream has imparted. My friend's dream occurred because she was worried about her A-levels.

The dream was her brain's way of urging her to take remedial action – perhaps by spending more time on studying and less time down the pub.

Strange Sleepers

Back to inventor Thomas Edison, who wasn't just a short sleeper, but also quite a strange one. He used particular sleep states as a tool to fuel his ingenuity.

Edison noticed that amazing insights would come to him while on the verge of sleep. This phenomenon is very real and is called Hypnagognia. It can be marked by odd thoughts, sounds and visions which occur as flashes and usually don't contain a narrative.

Hypnagognia happens when Alpha and Theta brain-waves overlap simultaneously, as our body is on the verge of drifting from relaxation into sleep.

Most people don't remember this state, as it occurs so briefly. But Edison did notice it and actively set out to prolong it. He would sit in a chair and relax while concentrating on something he wanted to gain more insight into. He held a set of metal balls in one hand, so that if he started to actually fall asleep, the balls would clatter to the ground. waking him up. He did this repeatedly until he was able to train his brain to stay in the hypnagogic state for longer periods. He, credited this method for his greatest breakthroughs.

But Edison wasn't the only oddball genius to use this technique. Surrealist painter Salvador Dali held a set of keys above a plate to wake himself when nodding off to sleep. He'd sit relaxing at his canvas when he felt sleepy, and then immediately start painting when the keys hit the plate.

If you want to tap into this altered state of mind and consciousness without doing anything quite so weird, meditation, biofeedback and hypnosis could all help you to access different mixtures of brainwaves.

While Leonardo da Vinci is most famous for his art, he sketched out and created prototypes for thousands of inventions, many of which were adopted by others later and made real. He was also famed for his odd sleep schedule, which involved a series of 20-minute to two-hour naps, which over 24 hours would give him roughly five hours of sleep. It was supposed that he did this to remain productive, but that sort of broken sleep can also lead to lucid dreaming, similar in some ways to Hypnagogia.

Sleeping for short periods throughout the day (called polyphasic sleep) can make you more productive if you can adapt to it. Another bright proponent of it was 'Bucky' Fuller, an architect, writer and inventor who published more than 30 books and held the post of World President of Mensa for almost a decade.

Bucky's main driver was contributing as much as he could to society by finding ways of doing more with less, so that more people could benefit. He applied the same principle to his sleep schedule. Bucky would work until he grew tired, which was roughly every six hours, then nap for 30 minutes, in order to give himself "22 hours of thinking time" per day.

There are many modern versions of the polyphasic sleep model, such as the Uberman and Everyman schedules. It should be noted that some of these are very restrictive in the amount of total hours of sleep, while others are more relaxed.

I can't claim to know the impact that polyphasic sleep might have on your health over a long period of time, especially if you are severely restricting your hours. But most people who do any form of it tend to take breaks and have a good, long sleep every few weeks. Others use it as a tool for a set amount of time when they have something important to accomplish.

There may be greater benefits – and fewer risks – to

adopting a biphasic sleep pattern (i.e. separating your sleep into two slots). Many primates live on a biphasic sleep schedule, and people in hot countries get by perfectly well taking a snooze, or *siesta*, after lunch. A lot of Mediterraneans live to a ripe old age, so there is no evidence to suggest that a shorter sleep and an afternoon nap will harm you in any way.

In fact, some historians and researchers have claimed that biphasic sleep is our natural way of sleeping. Records from history show that splitting sleep into two may have been the norm in the dark ages. Studies also indicate that when removed from artificial light, people naturally adopt biphasic sleep, especially in winter months when daylight is in short supply.

Some people maintain that this sort of sleep schedule helps to regulate stress, which you know by now is a brain-drainer. Some large businesses, including Ben & Jerrys, Uber, Google and Nike, encourage employees to take regular naps, claiming it keeps their workforce productive, happy, creative and resilient.

Your Ideal Sleep Schedule

You can retrain your body's rhythms to sleep any way you want to. But if you're making drastic changes, it will take time to adjust and you'll likely feel tired and slow for the first few days or weeks. If you want, or need, to change your Circadian rhythms so you can sleep during the day, get some blackout blinds, so you aren't woken up by the sun. It is hard to stay asleep when daylight floods through the curtains.

If you don't want to get too experimental, but just want to ensure that you're getting the best amount of sleep for you, you can work out how much sleep you need at this period of your life. It's quick and easy to do this. All you need is a bed and two consecutive days when you can wake up any time you want.

On the first day, go to bed when you feel tired and allow yourself to wake up naturally. If you've been deprived of rest, your body may sleep longer. On the second day, do the same thing, but this time note the last time you remember being awake before sleeping, then note the time you woke up.

The second natural sleep should give you an idea of how long you need to sleep for, since the results won't be skewed by not sleeping enough before.

If you are sleeping in past the time you usually have to start the day, go to bed a little earlier each night until you have shifted your sleep quota into its ideal slot, so that you wake up naturally at the time your alarm would usually ring.

Strrrrreeetttttch

If you've had enough sleep, you should remember what I said in the last chapter about positive self-appraisal making you happier and smarter. People who are confident in their abilities are more likely to succeed at anything they turn their hands to.

Forty percent of people sleep in the foetal position. While your partner may enjoy the extra room in the bed, sleeping like that can make you feel less capable when you wake up. Curling up tightly sends a signal to the brain saying we feel sensitive and unsafe, while postures which take up more space tell our brains we are confident. So, if you're sleeping all night in a ball, you're likely to wake up feeling low.

Try spreading yourself out more when you sleep. You can either sleep on your back or front to do this, or let your arms and legs spread wider across the bed.

If you can't get to sleep in any of these ways, you can counter the foetal position's effects by having a good stretch in the morning. Lift your chin, stand with your legs apart and stick your arms out. This stance will release chemicals to make you feel more confident.

To conclude, there are many ways that you can vary your sleep and tap into its different stages to become more creative, efficient and possibly even have some strokes of genius. But whatever you do, remember your health comes first.

Your body needs to fulfil your personal sleep quota in order to keep vital systems running, such as your nervous system and your endocrine system. A poorly functioning body hampers your physical and mental performance, so always check in with your body to make sure it's happy with what you're doing.

You'll know if it's not because you will feel drained, ill and torpid. And you certainly won't be feeling very sharp mentally either. We are all individuals, so your body may love or loathe some of the sleep cycles I have mentioned. By all means test them out, but if they just don't suit you, then accept it. This book is full of so many methods of boosting your brainpower that you don't need to resort to drastic sleep measures to be smarter.

Be wise – the sleep schedule that will make you smart is whichever one makes you feel rested, refreshed and on the ball when you wake.

Mirror, Mirror

Mirror, mirror on the wall, who's the smartest of them all? The person who looks at things from many angles and reflects on what they have learned to create smart solutions. That was a long answer.

One of the crucial keys to wisdom that recurs through this book is the ability to garner various perspectives. From Socratic questioning, to looking through a third party's eyes, to seeing things like a child would, new vistas help our minds to become broader and increase our likelihood of achieving success.

Whether you're trying to deal with a personal or work problem, or you are working on a project, a dream, a goal, or an idea, a fresh pair of eyes is always handy.

As a child, you'd never have learned to improve your work if you hadn't received it back with incorrect answers crossed in red ink. Or, if you had my teacher, a sad-looking face next to the bits I'd done wrong.

You would have carried on making the same mistakes and wouldn't have seen how you could make your work better. Or, if you had my teacher, you'd have never received a smiley face at the end of the page.

Generally, the more perspectives you can gather on something, the better your chances of getting a nice range of viewpoints and collecting more resources to help you on your way.

So, in this chapter we're going to deliberately ask for those red ticks, crosses and suggestions. We'll look at how to get great feedback so you can evaluate, adjust and improve your ideas and solutions.

People give feedback in many different ways, which is really rather helpful. Some will simply give you a personal opinion, while others may point out things you never noticed. Others might give you contacts or tips on other places to look for useful information and tools to help you make progress. Some people may even offer to help you directly if they like your ideas.

If you never reach out to other people, you could miss out on important data, valuable advice, resources, or even mentoring.

Never be afraid to ask for feedback. Most people like to help others if they can. And if anyone thinks your ideas or dreams are totally crazy, they are more likely to tell you so politely than to call you a complete nut-job (n.b. There are exceptions to this rule. Simon

Cowell, I'm talking about you).

Ask The Right People

As a writer of books, articles, academic papers, and fiction (I have a pen name for that, and no, it's not Dan Brown), I would be lost without feedback from other people. I always ask someone else about my ideas, to check my science or my wording, or to read my stories to see if they are any good. It's not always the same people, obviously. Whoever I ask must have either relevant knowledge or a keen interest in that particular area to get really helpful feedback.

One tip from the business world is to always hang around people who are smarter than you are, so that you can learn from them. The same rule isn't absolute regarding getting feedback, although it is helpful to include wise people when you want to check out the viability of your ideas.

But brainboxes are not the only people you should ask for their viewpoint. Children are not necessarily 'smarter' than you, but their feedback could be just as valuable because they see things differently.

And sometimes friends are the best people to give you advice on personal matters, since they are likely to know your character pretty well. The most useful perspectives will depend on your precise situation.

If you've got a business idea and are about to invest money in it, it makes sense to get the opinions of an experienced mogul before you take the leap. But you will also want to question potential customers to see if it's something they would buy. If there is no market, then all the business advice in the world will not help.

Imagine you've written a romance novel and want to know if it's any good. You don't have to ask a brainiac whether they like it or not. You simply need to ask people who enjoy reading romances.

And later on, if you want to your book to be bought by a major publisher, you will have to send it to an agent to see if they believe it has a chance of success. Their feedback will be of a different kind than that of a reader. An agent will consider whether your novel is commercial enough to publish and whether you need an editor to help you hone your craft. Of course, they will have their own personal opinions on the story too – people don't become agents if they hate reading. So, an agent can actually offer you multiple perspectives.

If you do desperately want an agent, then it is critical

to take their feedback on board, because they are the people who sell books to publishers. However, you only have to consider their advice seriously. You don't always have to take it. Agents aren't always right and they vary in their opinions. So if one agent won't take on your book, that doesn't mean another agent won't.

Even the final gatekeepers, publishing houses, can get it terribly wrong. *Harry Potter* might never have been published if it weren't for an eight-year-old girl.

Author J.K. Rowling did secure an agent for the first book in the series, but her agent was unable to sell the story to any publishing houses. Twelve publishers rejected the manuscript and a thirteenth was about to say "no" when a little girl changed all that. Just as a Bloomsbury editor was telling Ms. Rowling to get a day job, rather than wasting her time writing about wizards, the publishers' chairman asked his daughter, Alice, to read the first chapter of the book. The eight-year-old lapped it up and begged for the rest of the story. So, Bloomsbury decided to publish *Harry Potter* after all, and Ms. Rowling has made millions from wasting her time writing about wizards.

So, whatever you are looking for feedback on, you don't have to take everything others' say as gospel. The reason for asking for feedback is just to get other points of view. There is one exception to this...

The Wisdom Of The Crowd

Let's go back to the 'Flying Tailor' to demonstrate this because, while his story is tragic, it's also a little bit funny. Oh, come on, it is.

Franz Reichelt did ask for experts' feedback about the viability of his 'parachute suit'. And he should have listened when they said it would never work, because the experts were totally right. It didn't work. In fact, it was a lethal contraption.

Reichelt should also have taken the feedback from the hordes of people around the Eiffel Tower, urging him not to test the suit on himself. Because, again, they were completely right. His decision to jump was utter folly. He hadn't even successfully tested his latest design on a dummy, so the man was just dicing with death when he used himself as a tester.

Not just one, but a group of aeronautics experts, had all told Reichelt that his idea wouldn't fly. And not one, but a massive crowd of people, including friends, experts and unbiased strangers, told him not to jump.

If the feedback you have been given is all exactly the

same and comes from multiple perspectives, then you should take it very seriously.

Negative feedback doesn't necessarily mean you have to shelve your ideas, but it's a pretty strong signal that you should go back to the drawing board.

How To Get Good Feedback

It is vital to have relevant sources of feedback. As we saw with *Harry Potter*, almost all of the publishers had missed one indispensable point of view – that of a child. Call me crazy, but if I wanted to check whether or not children would like a book, I'd probably ask a bunch of kids to read it, rather than a panel of old men wearing tweed.

So, before asking just anyone for their point of view, consider who could give you the most relevant and valuable feedback.

First, make a list of the best groups or types of people to approach. Choose at least five categories to ensure you have a good spectrum of perspectives.

For example, if you're stuck on a relationship issue, your list might look like this:

BETH BURGESS

1. People who are in long-lasting relationships
2. Relationship experts
3. Friends who know me well
4. People who have experienced the same issue
5. People who know my partner well

Next, choose at least three people to approach within each category. If possible, pick a range of people, to get even broader perspectives. So, within the category of relationship experts, you might pick an agony aunt, a relationship counsellor, and a self-help author who writes about love.

Exactly how you approach different types of people will vary. With very good friends, you'd probably tell them your issue and ask for their advice outright. But what about people who know your partner? Asking them directly about the situation could really rock the boat, especially if they prefer your partner over you!

So, instead, tap into their knowledge of your partner's character. Having that extra information could still help you to make better decisions, even if you don't directly ask about the problem you are facing. You are still benefiting from a different perspective and more data you can use when making choices. You could learn some crucial stuff about your partner that helps with your decision, without even talking about the issue at hand.

When making your list, remember that you can get different sorts of feedback and data from different categories of people. You don't have to ask all of them the same questions. You can fit what you ask them to the most useful aspect of their perspective.

Even within categories, when you have identified the individuals you want to approach, you might find it useful to ask them for different types of feedback. If one of your friends is great at empathising, you could ask them what they would do if they were in your shoes. If another pal knows you inside out, you could ask them: "What do you think would be the right decision for me, personally?"

If you're not sure precisely what to ask a particular person, don't limit your scope by asking very specific questions. Instead, present them with the situation and simply ask: "What do you think?" This gives the individual the chance to offer their best advice. They might give you a list of pros and cons to certain decisions or tell you about a similar situation they were able to resolve. If you pick good sources, they will attempt to answer your question in the way they think will be most helpful and from the best of their experience and perspective.

You might not know some of the people on your list on a personal level. For example, you may not be acquainted with any expert authors. So how do you go about getting their advice? This will involve some cold contact, but you can warm it up a little before you begin by getting in touch online. Follow them on social media comment on their articles. Get on their radar before making direct contact. Then, when you write to them, you may seem familiar and they'll be more likely to reply. And if you're reading their stuff, you'll get gems of relevant advice anyway, which will instantly give you a better insight into your issue.

Your actual query letter should start with a positive comment on something they have written, done or said. Be specific. Don't just say: "I love your stuff". Say: "Your advice on X in Y book was excellent".

Next, keep your message as short as possible. People are busy these days and you're asking this person a favour, so don't make them wade through a lot of text in order to help you.

While you should be polite, it rarely hurts to inject a bit of humour into your writing if you can. Most people appreciate a little light-heartedness. I don't mean telling them jokes, but rather wording things in an engaging and amusing way.

I'll give you a successful example that I used when cold-contacting someone quite prestigious who I had never met or spoken to.

As well as the Wiseism series, I write books that focus on addiction and recovery. When I wrote my first book, *The Recovery Formula*, I knew I needed feedback from addiction experts. So I wrote to someone famous in the field. He had a column in a national newspaper, had founded a rehab centre, and had published 26 books of his own. I learned a little more about him and realised he was a former addict, so I used that in my message too.

I wrote a short, but sweet, email and attached a PDF of the book. I started off with a bit of flattery about a video he had made. It wasn't fake – you should never go there – I genuinely admired the way he presented his views on addiction.

Then I wrote something like: "I know this is totally cheeky, but seeing as you're the don of recovery, I have to ask: would you mind having a flick through a book I've written? I am an alkie myself – a sober one, of course. Otherwise nothing in the book would have made sense. In fact, I wouldn't have written a book.

I'd be lying in a bush somewhere rather than asking you to please have a little look at my book and tell me whether you think it's any good."

Not only did I get a positive response to my email, but I got invited out to lunch so he could give me more encouragement, because he actually loved the book. And then, he agreed to write an endorsement for it as well. And I made a new friend. Bonus! Reaching out in the right way can really pay off when you're dealing with people you don't (yet) know.

Now, who have we forgotten in this quest for good feedback? No, not your Auntie Marge, as great as her advice may be. Take a look in the mirror. We haven't mentioned *you* yet...

Reflect And Correct

Your own feedback can be so valuable. I'm not talking about those useless self-reviews that work may force you to do. When I wasn't self-employed, I had to do those and I always found them an utter waste of time.

I was always a really hard worker and took on jobs suited to my skills, so there genuinely wasn't much to improve on. So I made things up to fill in the boxes. I even wrote in huge letters just to fill up more space.

And I felt it was arrogant to go on about what I was good at, so I would give myself lower ratings than I really deserved, so that I didn't look like a big-head. So, my work self-reviews were completely inaccurate and didn't teach me anything or give me any goals to work on at all.

But genuine reflection can give you amazing insights. Many colleges ask students to write out a reflection after doing certain exercises. They ask you to include things you have noticed about your character, and the way you approach things as well as what you learned directly related to the task at hand.

Reflecting like that is a really useful way of creating your own feedback and giving yourself new targets and things to work on. Deep reflection can even drive you in a totally fresh direction, as you realise things that you hadn't before.

You can use reflection at any point in your life to work out where you're going – or where you've been going wrong.

Reflection is also helpful when you have just had a new experience or encounter and want to know what it really *gave* you or how you could improve things in your next interaction. It's perfect after a job interview or for a post-date post-mortem.

A wise way to use reflection is to cement and expand your learning. When you've learned something new, use reflection to consider different applications for the knowledge you have acquired. How could it help you in other areas of your life? What would happen if you used similar principles in a different field? This can help you become truly innovative and discover smart new ways of doing things.

Reflection is also a wonderful tool to use when you're working towards a goal, be it a specific project or a more general one, such as being a better person.

If you're really into it, you could use it on a daily or weekly basis, to see what you have learned during that period about the world and about yourself. It can literally make you wiser each time you do it.

Regular reviews can help you achieve greater balance in your life and also ensure you're making steady progress with who you want to be and what you want to do. It can also cue you to change your attitude and behaviours if you can clearly see they aren't doing you any good.

So, how do you do it? Firstly, you must promise to be

totally honest with yourself. You will not gloss over any difficult things you discover, nor diminish any achievements you have made. No-one else is going to see or judge your reflections, so you can be totally open and candid with your thoughts.

Secondly, this is not the Spanish Inquisition nor an exercise in beating yourself up if you haven't done as well as you would've hoped. Rather, it's an extra learning opportunity, so if you aren't on the right path, you can correct that.

Thirdly, to reflect effectively, you must look at your experience from a variety of angles. So, look at the bigger picture as well as zooming in on the details. Don't make mountains out of molehills, nor minimise problems or challenges. Think of how other people fit into events. Analyse the relationships between things, so you can see where a cause leads to a certain effect. By examining things from different perspectives, you will end up with a deeper, truer, and more balanced reflection.

Once you have understood the attitude needed for reflection – namely, openness, honesty, perspective, positivity, learning, and gentle correction – then you are ready to begin. So, grab a piece of paper and find a private, quiet place to do your reflection.

Question Yourself

The questions you will ask yourself will depend on what you're using your reflection for. I've already given you a couple to use if you're trying to cement and amplify new learning.

The basic questions to use after doing tasks are: What did I learn through doing this task? What did I learn about myself? What did I do well? What could I have done better?

There is little point in pointing out your weaknesses and leaving it at that. If you could have improved on things, then set yourself a target that will help you next time. Be honest about your abilities and how quickly you can change. If you think it will be hard to improve, write down one realistic step you can take to move forwards. You can add further steps once you've achieved the first. It is fine to take your time if things are particularly difficult. Progress is the name of the game.

If you're evaluating your performance on a task or trying to work out a project, double-questions will get you to the heart of the matter. So, don't just ask: "What didn't work?" Also ask: "Why not?" Equally, asking: "What worked – and why?" is much more helpful than just noting down what worked.

You can add any questions you like to your reflection. You may need to ask some questions that are specific to what you're reflecting on. If you are carrying out a general reflection, here are some interesting questions you might like to include:

What have I learned about the world today?

How has my attitude helped and/or hindered me?

What impact have my actions had on other people?

What am I most/least proud of about myself?

What was the most meaningful thing I did this week?

If I could do today again, what would I change?

What should I do more/less of to achieve my goals?

What has been today's most valuable lesson?

How could I have made things easier for myself?

What do I most urgently need to change?

What could I have done to be happier this week?

What, precisely, is the progress I have made today?

If you can't answer the last one, then write down the next step you will take to make some progress.

When you are reflecting on aspects of yourself, be it your behaviour, attitude, or character, the goal is not only to become more self-aware, but also to alter any aspects that are holding you back.

Reflect On Your Reflection

When you have reflected deeply, poured your heart out, and investigated every aspect of your soul, sit for a moment and make sure there isn't anything you're refusing to admit or blocking out.

If you feel like you've genuinely covered everything, read your reflection back. As you go through it, draw stars by anything especially positive, including new insights, and put numbers by anything you need to change. Then, run through the numbers, and at the end of the page, make a corresponding list of what you are going to do to improve. Finally, sign it, like a contract, because that's what it is – a contract with yourself.

There is no point in saying "Oh, my selfishness really didn't help me out there" and then doing nothing to become more thoughtful about others. If you want to be truly wise, you have to be committed to changing unhelpful aspects of your character.

It is always worth developing yourself and acquiring better qualities, because it will make your life a lot easier in the end. While it may take some work, you will never regret the effort, because your negative aspects hinder you in so many critical ways. They can cause rifts in your relationships, close many doors to you, and stop you from reaching your goals.

You can try your very first feedback session right now by reflecting on what you have learned and found out about yourself in the course of reading this book. How has it changed your perspective? What goals are you going to set yourself so you can instantly be smarter and develop your wisdom?

So, that's it for feedback. I hope it's been helpful. If it hasn't, naturally I want to know why not. So feel free to send me your own feedback, good or bad. Send it to me at beth@wiseism.com. Just don't type it in green ink, or I might think you're a bit of a fruitcake (or maybe you're just a free spirit). Let me know what else you'd like to learn. What would you like me to cover more deeply?

If you've got positive feedback, please leave me a nice review on your favourite online bookstore, telling me what was most helpful and why. Let me know what you've managed to achieve using the methods in this book. I love to hear readers' success stories :)

Don't Miss This!

You've already seen, and hopefully experienced, how being wiser can improve your life in many ways. I'm always deepening my learning and I hope you want to as well. This book is just the beginning and your potential is unlimited. If you want to continue your journey with me, then **choose wisdom**.

I have a lot more to share with you, so if you'd like to stay connected...

Visit Wiseism: www.wiseism.com

Follow Wiseism on Twitter:
https://twitter.com/WiseismTweets

Like Wiseism on Facebook:
https://www.facebook.com/Wiseism.Wisdom

And as a HUGE THANK YOU for reading my book, I'm giving you a special gift absolutely free.

I've mentioned my book *How to Create Your Ideal Life* a few times for a reason. I'm giving you a head-start on everyone else. To get the first part free, just sign up here: https://signup.ymlp.com/xgbusqqbgmgus

Here's to wisdom :)

www.ingramcontent.com/pod-product-compliance
Lightning Source LLC
Chambersburg PA
CBHW051424090426
42737CB00014B/2822